Sixth Workshop on Natural Language and Computer Science (NLCS 2019)

Gothenburg, Sweden
24 May 2019

ISBN: 978-1-5108-9095-4

Printed from e-media with permission by:

Curran Associates, Inc.
57 Morehouse Lane
Red Hook, NY 12571

Some format issues inherent in the e-media version may also appear in this print version.

Printed by Curran Associates, Inc. (2019)

For permission requests, please contact the Association for Computational Linguistics at the address below.

Association for Computational Linguistics
209 N. Eighth Street
Stroudsburg, Pennsylvania 18360

Phone: 1-570-476-8006
Fax: 1-570-476-0860

acl@aclweb.org

Additional copies of this publication are available from:

Curran Associates, Inc.
57 Morehouse Lane
Red Hook, NY 12571 USA
Phone: 845-758-0400
Fax: 845-758-2633
Email: curran@proceedings.com
Web: www.proceedings.com

TABLE OF CONTENTS

PREFACE

NLCS 2019, the Sixth Workshop on Natural Language and Computer Science was held in Gothenburg, Sweden on May 24, 2019. NLCS'19 was a workshop held as part of the The 13th International Conference on Computational Semantics (IWCS 2019). It was also endorsed by SIGSEM.

NLCS attracts papers from a wide range of areas connected to computer science. A few of those areas: logic for semantics of lexical items, sentences, discourse and dialog; continuations in natural language semantics; formal tools in textual inference, such as logics for natural language inference; applications of category theory in semantics; linear logic in semantics; and formal approaches to unifying data-driven and declarative approaches to semantics.

More on NLCS, including links to previous editions, may be found at `http://www.indiana.edu/~iulg/nlcs.html`.

This year, we received six submissions and accepted four. This is the first collocation with IWCS, and we were pleased to work with the conference. We thank all of the organizers of IWCS, especially Simon Dobnik and Asad Sayeed, for their very considerable help with our meeting, especially in preparing this volume

We thank our Program Committee for their hard work in reading and reporting on all of our submissions. The PC consisted of Dag Haug (University of Oslo), Aurelie Herbelot (University of Trento), Makoto Kanazawa (Hosei University), Gerald Penn (University of Toronto), Kyle Richardson (Allen Institute for Artificial Intelligence), and the three co-chairs.

We are grateful to our two invited speakers. Rafaella Bernardi spoke on "Grounding language into vision incrementally and without forgetting." Krasimir Angelov spoke on "WordNet as an Interlingual Translation Lexicon." Both talks were wonderful additions to our meeting.

We would like to thank the authors of the papers in this special issue for their excellent submissions and talks.

Robin Cooper, Valeria de Paiva, and Lawrence S. Moss
PC Co-Chairs

Distribution is not enough: going Firther

Andy Lücking
University Paris-Diderot, Goethe University Frankfurt
luecking@em.uni-frankfurt.de

Robin Cooper
Gothenburg University
robin.cooper@ling.gu.se

Staffan Larsson
Gothenburg University
staffan.larsson@ling.gu.se

Jonathan Ginzburg
University Paris-Diderot
yonatan.ginzburg@univ-paris-diderot.fr

Abstract

Much work in contemporary computational semantics follows the *distributional hypothesis* (DH), which is understood as an approach to semantics according to which the meaning of a word is a function of its distribution over contexts which is represented as vectors (word embeddings) within a multi-dimensional semantic space. In practice, use is identified with occurrence in text corpora, though there are some efforts to use corpora containing multi-modal information.

In this paper we argue that the distributional hypothesis is *intrinsically* misguided as a *self-supporting basis* for semantics, as Firth was entirely aware. We mention philosophical arguments concerning the lack of normativity within DH data. Furthermore, we point out the shortcomings of DH as a model of learning, by discussing a variety of linguistic classes that cannot be learnt on a distributional basis, including indexicals, proper names, and wh-phrases. Instead of pursuing DH, we sketch an account of the problematic learning cases by integrating a rich, Firthian notion of dialogue context with interactive learning in signalling games backed by in probabilistic Type Theory with Records. We conclude that the success of the DH in computational semantics rests on a *post hoc* effect: DS presupposes a referential semantics on the basis of which utterances can be produced, comprehended and analysed in the first place.

1 Introduction

Much work in contemporary computational semantics follows the *distributional hypothesis* (DH), attributed to Harris (1954) and Firth (1957), which is understood as an approach to semantics according to which the meaning of a word is a function of its distribution over contexts which is represented as vectors (word embeddings) within a multi-dimensional semantic space. In practice, use is identified with occurrence in text corpora, though there are some efforts to use corpora containing multi-modal information (e.g Bruni et al., 2014). The appealing prospect of distributional semantics (DS) is to provide a *self-supporting semantic theory* according to which semantic representations can be bootstrapped from corpora in an entirely empirical fashion:

> Word space models constitute a purely descriptive approach to semantic modelling; it does not require any previous linguistic or semantic knowledge, and it only detects what is actually there in the data. (Sahlgren, 2005, p. 3)

In this paper we argue that the distributional hypothesis is intrinsically misguided as a self-supporting basis for semantics (for such a claim, see Baroni et al. (2014); also Baroni and Lenci (2010) argue in that direction), as—somewhat surprisingly—Firth was entirely aware. Note that our discussion points at reference and interaction as semantic building blocks, not to inferential and compositional properties which are often mentioned as motivating factors behind engaging in *Formal Distributional Semantics* (FDS; Boleda and Herbelot, 2016) or distributional probabilistic inference (Erk, 2016). In section 2 we begin with mentioning pertinent philosophical arguments concerning the lack of normativity within DH data due to McGinn (1989) (and with reservations Kripke 1982). These argument show that collections of past uses do not allow to deduce a notion of veridicality, since the regularities within any collection of data do not project to semantic norms. Using supervised models (where target data or a so-called 'ground truth' are spelled out in advance), DS might try to implement normative knowledge nonetheless. But this move amounts to a circular approach: semantic knowledge is needed in order to apply distributional semantic methods in the first place. Thus, we observe a *bootstrapping problem* here. This problem is conceded within DS in general: 'The results suggest that, while distributional semantic vectors can be used "as-is" to capture generic word similarity, with some supervision it is also possible to extract other kinds of information from them [...]' (Gupta et al., 2015, p. 20). Obviously, the bootstrapping problem completely undermines the DH's claim to provide a semantic theory. However, work that aims at accounting for such 'higher order' phenomena in distributional terms but drawing on additional resources or annotations—like Herbelot and Vecchi (2015), who map distributional information onto quantified sentences, Gupta et al. (2015), who map distributions to knowledge base information, or Aina et al. (2018), who employ distributional semantics on character annotations within a specifically designed network model—puts its emphasis not on distributional semantic representation, but on how to *learn* these representations. We observe a further, *de facto* construal of DH here, a construal that draws on the notion of supervised learning, triggered by the procedures of data extraction or machine learning. Accordingly, in section 3 we discuss a variety of linguistic classes that cannot be learnt on the basis of the distributional hypothesis, including indexicals (Oshima-Takane et al., 1999), proper names (Herbelot, 2015), and wh-phrases. In section 5 we sketch an account of these problematic cases that integrates a rich notion of dialogue context (Ginzburg, 2012) with interactive learning in signalling games backed by a probabilistic Type Theory with Records (Cooper et al., 2015), which lays the foundations for spreading probabilities over situations.

This diagnosis of DS can be related to two different notions of semantics as a theory of meaning (cf. Lewis, 1970, p. 19). , namely semantic theory as a specification of the meanings of words and sentences (vector spaces), and a foundational theory of meaning identify the facts in virtue of which words and sentences do have the meaning they have (learning) We point at struggles of the DH with both of these respects here. We will even, for the most part, put aside one of the intrinsic issues confronting the DH—the *sentential denotation issue*: how to get distributional vectors to denote/represent/correspond to events or propositions or questions. Nor do we deal with compositionality. We deal primarily with lexical semantic issues (though not entirely, given the discussion of wh-phrases ...).

2 Philosophical Arguments against the distributional hypothesis in a nutshell

The normativity argument is as simple as powerful: since not every language use is a correct one, you want to partition uses into correct and incorrect ones. However, as ascertained by McGinn (1989, p. 160), 'this partitioning cannot be effected without employing a notion not definable simply from the notion of bare use'. That is, use falls short of capturing veridical normativity.[1]

Thus, the distributional hypothesis as pursued in computational semantics (textual or multimodal) fails to account for *semantic normativity*. Following teleological reasoning in philosophy of language (which takes off with Millikan, 1984) we suggest that meaning does not just reside in mere use, but is learned by trial and error under the pressure of coordination, as is partly simulated within evolutionary game theory. However, based on discussing three particular linguistic phenomena (Sec. 3), we further

[1]There is a second argument against usage-based semantics, which appeals to the problem of induction: Kripke (1982, Sec. 2) argues that use does not fix the extension of the reference relation by example of 'quus' and 'plus'. 'Quus' and 'plus' are two different arithmetic functions which have the same value up to a certain point but diverge thereafter. Having only observed uses of '+' up to the point of divergence, why should you refer by '+' to 'plus' and not to 'quus'? However, this argument is convincing only when fixed extensions are assumed, as is usually done in the closed models of formal semantics. A classifier-based semantics (Larsson, 2015), which is embraced by the authors, is compatible to open models and therefore takes Kripke's argument as further evidence that extensions indeed are not fixed.

argue with Firth that semantic games have to couched in an interaction based ontology (Sec.4).

3 Linguistic Evidence against the distributional hypothesis

To the more philosophical concerns (which alone point to the difficulties of taking DH in some form as the basis for semantic theory) we ground our case with three classes of linguistic expressions, all of which are pervasive in conversation and that seem to resist a distributional analysis, namely *indexicals*, *proper names*, and *wh-words*. Indexicals and proper names involve the issue of *semantic denseness*: they occur in too many places to have distinctive neighbours; this, arguably also afflicts wh-phrases, though they have distinctive syntactic positions in some languages.

An NLP adherent, who cares not about cognitive concerns, could argue for indexicals and wh-phrases that these need to be hard-wired in (and added as dimensions in the vector space) and that a distributional semantics deals with the lexical dynamics of a mature learner. This does not work so well for proper names, but once again one could claim that these are hard-wired in as independent dimensions (the entity libraries used by Aina et al. 2018 come close to this approach) and then new items learnt by analogy. But in any case, they would need to demonstrate that the emergent semantics could deal with the (dialogical) context dependence and perspectivity of all these expressions, which vector representations do not, at present at least, offer a solution to.

3.1 Indexicals

Examples of indexical expressions are the first and second person singular pronouns *I* and *you*. What does it take to acquire the corresponding semantic rules? Moyer et al. (2015, p. 2) are explicit in this regard: 'Thus, to achieve adult-like competence, the child must infer on the basis of the input, that *I* marks speaker, *you* marks addressee, and *s/he* marks a salient individual, usually a non-participant. To do so, she must pay attention to the discourses in which pronouns are used, specifically at each given moment, who is speaking, who is being addressed, and who is participating (or not) in the conversation.' The dialogue role-awareness is crucial in order for children to acquire the capacity of reversal necessary for the mastery of indexical pronouns, a difficulty ascertained by Oshima-Takane et al. (1999). That is, in case of indexical pronouns it is precisely not their co-occurrence pattern that give clues to their reference, but their relation to contextual indices. A learning game for pronouns that follows closely these psycholinguistic lines is designed in Sec. 5.1.

3.2 Proper names

With regard to proper names there is the notorious difficulty to separate named entity vectors from common noun vectors. This can only be achieved by employing additional processing on top of a distributional analysis like named entity recognition within a domain of uniquely named individuals (Herbelot, 2015; the need of additional preprocessing is also admitted by Baroni et al., 2014, p. 260, if one wants to distinguish proper names from common nouns at all). However, it is difficult to see how this unique description approach to proper names within distributional semantics (DS) can be applied to 'real-world' data where one and the same proper name word form (say, *John*) refers to many different individuals, intuitively, that individual that is jointly known by that name to the interlocutors. A very standard naming game that gives rise to polysemous names, but employs two vocabularies, is sketched in Sec. 5.2.

3.3 wh-words

With wh-words we reach a new difficulty that, in contrast to indexicals and proper names, they are not referential. Wh-words are used to from questions or initiate relative clauses. When used to form a question, a wh-word (like *which?* or *who?*) can address nearly any constituent or referent of the preceding text. In terms of distributions, wh-words therefore stand out due to contextual promiscuity.

What is lost is their indication of illocutionary force (question marking), which seems to be a key aspect.[2] Furthermore, wh-words can request implicit referents, that is, referents that lack a surface realisation.

An example being *A: I found an earring yesterday. B: Where?*, where B queries the location of the finding situation, which is not verbalised. Since DS operates on surface co-occurrence, any implicit referent (as any kind of elliptical construction) has to be regarded as theoretically problematic.[3]

4 Ontology

The phenomena discussed (indexicals, proper names, wh-words) rely on relations to constituents of the situation of utterance, contextual relations which Firth was fully aware of (cf. Firth, 1957, p. 5 f.). Firth distinguishes two main sets of relations: firstly, syntagmatic and paradigmatic relations; secondly situational relations, which include as a subset what he calls 'analytic relations':

> Analytic relations set up between parts of the text (words or parts of words, and indeed, any 'bits' or 'pieces'), and special constituents, items, objects, persons, or events within the situation. (Firth, 1957, p. 5, footnote omitted)

However, back in his time '[t]he technical language necessary for the description of contexts of situation is not developed' (Firth, 1957, p. 9).[4] This shortage has been remedied by contemporary semantic theory, in particular dialogue semantics. Therefore, we follow a more complete approach, as may have been envisaged by Firth, and employ a detailed context model (namely Ginzburg's (2012) KoS) in order to get a grip on indexicals, proper names, and *wh*-words. In this sense, we plead for 'going Firther' by incorporating the full range of contextual relations into semantic models. Very briefly, language use takes place in utterance situations which can be modelled in terms of *dialogue game boards*, that is, 'scoresheets' that keep track of participants, utterances and meanings (a very rudimentary example is provided in Sec.5.1 below—in fact, it is so rudimentary that it only hosts participants; utterances and meanings are recorded in the exchanges and utility functions of the accompanying game dynamics). Meanings are construed as *Austinian propositions* (going back to Austin, 1950 and adopted in situation semantics (Barwise and Perry, 1983)), pairs of situations and situations types (which will be crucial for accounting for indexicality in Sec.5.1). Similarly, following Ginzburg et al. (2014), we appeal to *Austinian questions* as pairs of situations and abstracts; their original motivation was a unified treatment of Boolean operations with propositions and an account of adjectival modification. Here, following Moradlou and Ginzburg (2014), we appeal to them as a means for conceptualizing how questions get acquired as a consequence of situationally grounded interaction. Thus, there are three kinds of semantic objects (*SemObj*), namely (objects in) situations (can also be understood as *frames*), Austinian propositions, and Austinian questions. Meanings then are mappings from utterance situations to SemObj and can be learned from aggregating experiences linking interactions in situations to SemObj. We sketch three scenarios thereof.

5 Learning lexical meanings

Using the ontology briefly exposited in the previous section, we sketch three learning scenarios for acquiring mastery of the meaning of the linguistic phenomena introduced in Sec. 3. Our strategy is to relate the ontological context model to game theory. Unlike Lazaridou et al. (2017), who aim at training agents in a game-theoretical setting, our motivation is theoretically driven by the semantic requirements to incorporate interaction and normativity. The respective learning task is operationalised in terms of agents' behaviour that, in the evolution of successful games, converge from random actions to utility-driven actions.

[2] wh-words also have embedded uses where the querying force is neutralized, an extra complication explicated by the semantic combinatorial mechanism.

[3] One might argue that distributions can still be obtained from annotated data where implicit referents are explicated. However, DS seems to be unable pull the required annotation off itself. So one needs a semantic analysis in order to get a distributional semantics to work in the first place—we identified this circularity as the bootstrapping problem in Sec. 1.

[4] On 'contexts of situation' see also Firth (1935, p. 64 ff.).

5.1 Pronoun games

Using singular pronouns properly depends on the speaker being a discourse participant or not, thus, it is intrinsically related to the utterance situation (this is the indexicality of first and second person singular pronoun). Regardless of which role a participant has in discourse, the first person pronoun refers to the speaker, the second person pronoun to the addressee and the third person one to some salient individual (bystander) different from speaker and addressee (assuming that *he* or *she* are used exophorically, that is, referring to an individual accessible in the utterance situation).

A child acquires the corresponding linguistic competence between one and three years (see the survey provided by Moyer et al., 2015, p. 2–3). This competence can be conceived as being acquired in 'pronoun games' that take place in different kinds of learning situations characterised by the discourse role and pronoun used. Let us assume a minimal example involving a tiny social network consisting of a child (girl) and its parents (say, traditional mother and father). The utterances that are produced in this situations are about someone being dirty, where someone is identified by one of three pronouns (for simplicity, we do not distinguish the gender of the third person pronoun (alternatively, one could assume a non-traditional family structure where just one third person is needed anyway)):

(1) a. 'I'm dirty.'
    b. 'You are dirty.'
    c. 'She/he is dirty.'

The declarative sentences from (1) give rise to Austinian propositions (cf. Sec. 4), namely that the situations thereby described are of the type claimed by the compositional derivation of the three word utterances. Let us further assume, that each participant has acquired a solid competence in judging an individual as being of type *dirty* in a situation (we assume for concreteness that this is accomplished by means of Bayesian learning in probabilistic TTR according to Cooper et al. (2015) exploiting perceptual classifications (Larsson, 2015).

Thus, the blueprint of the pronoun game is a situation of the following form, which is more or less the format of an utterance type in KoS (Ginzburg, 2012):

(2)
$$
\text{s} : \begin{bmatrix} \text{phon} & : & \langle\, \alpha \text{ am/are/is dirty} \,\rangle \\ \text{dgb-params} & : & \begin{bmatrix} \text{spkr} & : & \text{Ind} \\ \text{addr} & : & \text{Ind} \\ \text{bystander} & : & \text{Ind} \\ \text{s0} & : & \text{Rec} \\ \text{c1} & : & \text{addressing(spkr,addr)} \\ \text{c2} & : & \text{disengaged(}\big\{\text{spkr,addr}\big\}\text{, bystander)} \end{bmatrix} \\ \text{cont} & : & \begin{bmatrix} \text{sit} & = & \text{dgb-params.s0 : Rec} \\ \text{sit-type} & = & \begin{bmatrix} \text{x} & = & \begin{array}{l} \text{s.dgb-params.spkr} \vee \\ \text{s.dgb-params.addr} \vee \\ \text{s.dgb-params.bystander} \quad : \quad \text{Ind} \end{array} \\ \text{c}_\text{h} & : & \text{dirty(x)} \end{bmatrix} : \text{RecType} \end{bmatrix} \end{bmatrix}
$$

Given the schema in (2), the actual learning situation for a pronoun game is determined by randomly instantiating the discourse roles 'spkr', 'addr' and 'bystander' with a member of the social network (child, mother, father), and by assigning label x a value from the social network (i.e., s.dgb-params.spkr, s.dgb-params.addr, s.dgb-params.bystander), fixing who is dirty and is referred to.

Thus, given the modelling of Firthian 'contexts of situation' by means of modern dialogue semantics (Cooper, 2019; Ginzburg, 2012, and Sec. 4), all ingredients being there for engaging in a *Lewis game*

(Lewis, 1969), following standard game theory in semantics and pragmatics (Steels, 1997; Jäger, 2012). We construct such a game along the lines of Mühlenbernd and Franke (2012) by means of the following parameters:

- Social signals are exchanged between a *sender* (spkr) and a *receiver* (addr).
- Exchanges take place in a states $t_i \in T$, where each t_i is defined by assigning individuals to spkr, addr, and bystander ($3! = 6$, by combinatorics) and fixing x (3 possibilities). So the sample space T has $6 \times 3 = 18$ states to choose from. Since all have an equal chance to be chosen, the probability p for each $t_i \in T$ is $p(t_i) = \frac{1}{18} \approx 0.055$.
- The signals exchanged are messages $m \in \{I, you, she\}$, $p(m = I) = p(m = you) = p(m = she) = \frac{1}{3}$.
- Messages are responded to by an action $a \in \{I, you, she\}$, which, when effected by mother or father, amounts to parental feedback (amounting to answering 'right' or 'wrong').
- Players want to communicate successfully, so each participant has a utility function $u(t_i, a_j) = \begin{cases} 1 & \text{if } t_i = a_j \\ 0 & \text{otherwise} \end{cases}$

Current (and future) exchanges are informed by a history of successful, past interactions—in terms of a sender's belief about a receiver $B_r(a \mid m)$ and a receiver's belief about a sender $B(t \mid m)$—, stored in expected utility functions *EU* for both sender and receiver ((3) and (4) closely follow the functions defined by Mühlenbernd and Franke (2012)):

(3) a. $EU_s(m \mid t) = \sum_{a \in A} B_r(a \mid m) \times u(t, a)$

b. $EU_r(a \mid m) = \sum_{t \in T} B_s(t \mid m) \times u(t, a)$

A *best response strategy* σ for the sender (given a situation type t) and ρ for the receiver (given sender's message m) is to maximise their expected utilities. A standard method in order to compute this strategies is the arg max function:

(4) a. $\sigma(m \mid t) = \begin{cases} \frac{1}{\arg\max_m EU_s(m|t)} & \text{if } t \in \arg\max_m EU_s(m \mid t) \\ 0 & \text{else} \end{cases}$

b. $\rho(a \mid m) = \begin{cases} \frac{1}{\arg\max_a EU_r(a|m)} & \text{if } a \in \arg\max_a EU_r(a \mid m) \\ 0 & \text{else} \end{cases}$

In order to validate this model it is not even necessary to run a simulation study. The pronoun game employs a fixed vocabulary without homonyms and synonyms; each participant has equal chances to be assigned to the discourse roles; and the utility function acts as an amplifying function: such naming games are known to lead to lexical convergence (cf. De Vylder and Tuyls, 2006).[5] Since in our case the parents outnumber the child and therefore have greater impact on the expected utility functions, we can also predict which equilibrium will eventually be reached and characterise it with the lexical extracts in (5):[6]

[5] Readers might think of the pronoun games in terms of Pólya urns: each speaker has a urn associated with each type $t_i \in T$ that contains the n copies of the lexical elements of choice for denoting t_i (likewise for recipients). After a successful exchange took place, the number of copies of the successful lexical item will be increased by k, while the unsuccessful ones will be decreased by m ($n, i, k \in \mathbb{N}$ being parameters of the game). Thus, on the next turn, chances for converging on a lexical item increase already by number, and so on.

[6] Unless, of course, the parents entertain a private language where the meanings of the singular pronouns are interchanged in some way. But there will be lexical convergence in such a case, too.

(5) $$\left[\begin{array}{l} \text{phon} : \langle\ \text{i}\ \rangle \\ \text{dgb-params} : \left[\begin{array}{l}\text{spkr} : \text{Ind} \\ \text{addr} : \text{Ind} \\ \text{bystander} : \text{Ind}\end{array}\right] \\ \text{cont} : \left[\text{x=dgb.spkr} : \text{Ind}\right] \end{array}\right], \left[\begin{array}{l} \text{phon} : \langle\ \text{you}\ \rangle \\ \text{dgb-params} : \left[\begin{array}{l}\text{spkr} : \text{Ind} \\ \text{addr} : \text{Ind} \\ \text{bystander} : \text{Ind}\end{array}\right] \\ \text{cont} : \left[\text{x=dgb.addr} : \text{Ind}\right] \end{array}\right], \left[\begin{array}{l} \text{phon} : \langle\ \text{she/he}\ \rangle \\ \text{dgb-params} : \left[\begin{array}{l}\text{spkr} : \text{Ind} \\ \text{addr} : \text{Ind} \\ \text{bystander} : \text{Ind}\end{array}\right] \\ \text{cont} : \left[\text{x=dgb.bystander} : \text{Ind}\right] \end{array}\right]$$

That is, the pronoun *I* refers to the speaker of the utterance situation, *you* to the addressee and *she/he* to the bystander, irrespective whether the discourse roles are occupied by father, mother, or child.

In the implementation of Aina et al. (2018), which is related to our proposal, pronouns are learned from semantically annotated dialogue of character references (obtained from data of the TV series *Friends* of Chen and Choi 2016) by means of an LSTM with an *entity library*. The input data looks as follows, where numbers are IDs for characters:

> JOEY (183): '…see Ross (335), because I (183) think you (335) love her (306).'

The authors assume that 'the LSTM can learn to simply forward the speaker embedding unchanged in the case of pronoun *I*' (Aina et al., 2018, p. 68). But simply mapping *I* to whatever is left to the colon still misses perspectivity, which is the crucial issue about first and second person pronouns, cf. Moyer et al. (2015).

5.2 Proper names

At first glance, proper names seem to be the easiest part of speech to learn. Indeed, it is individual constants (predicate logic's formal device for representing proper names) that are learned in the most basic naming game scenarios (Lücking and Mehler, 2012). However, as briefly discussed in Sec. 3.2, proper names are homonymous expressions: one and the same name (understood as a word form) can apply to different individuals. In order to reflect this in a naming game, the assumption of a one-to-one correspondence between a word and an object has to be given up in favour of set-valued predicate constants. However, lifting proper names to polysemous terms clearly misses their point of being identificational expressions. Some semantic theories suggest to reconcile this conflict by analysing proper names as a hybrid of referential and descriptive expressions, where a proper name poses a presuppositional constraint on the individual referred to, which is (in a successful exchange) individuated by being mapped to a description (for such a semantic analysis see Cooper, 2019, Chap. 4). In order for agents of a naming game to learn such 'presuppositional names', we propose a two-stage game resting on two disjoint vocabularies: At the first stage, agents acquire possibly polysemous predicates by interchanging symbols from the first vocabulary. At the second stage, agents expands the $1 : m$-relations learned in the first level by means the second vocabulary. The second stage aims at capturing the descriptive content of proper names. We conjecture that the second stage could also be implemented in terms of grounding types by means of Bayesian learning (Cooper et al., 2015). In effect, agents acquire a second set of naming conventions which in most cases disambiguate the first set.[7] Granted, this is just the first step into the build-up of a long-term memory concerning named individuals (cf. Cooper 2019, Chap. 4; see also Weston et al. 2014).

Dialogically speaking, in this two-stage set-up agents acquire the equipment that partly corresponds to exchanges like the following: A: Sam was injured. B: Which one? A: The fireman. What is missing is the learning of wh-question (and answering them), to which we turn now.

5.3 Wh-words

Moradlou and Ginzburg (2014) sketch an account of how question understanding emerges. They identify a three-stage process:

[7] There may still be ambiguity left, but this also happens in real life and indicates that still further descriptive information have to be gathered in some cases.

1. Salient Object Identification games: a question is asked prompting for an appropriate descriptor of an object presented to the child.
2. Erotetically Plausible question games (EPQ) games: a question is asked in a situation where an obvious question arises.
3. Situational Description (SD) games: a question is asked about properties of objects observable in the situation.

Stages 1 and 2 habituate the child to associate wh-words with the need to consider possible resolutions of questions. In stage 1 the hypothesis space ranges over properties of objects. In stage 2 the hypothesis space is broadened to other aspects of the situation. The required SemObj become available due to the semantic ontology employed (cf. Sec. 4).

Wh-word competence ultimately consists in the identification of the queried domain and recognition that a question is being posed. Our basic conjecture is

(6) Conjecture: the sequence SOI–EPQ–SD leads to the emergence of wh-word competence.

We discuss here the first stage of this sequence, namely SOI games. An SOI game can be implemented on top of a two-stage naming game as sketched in Sec. 5.2. When an interaction in terms of a word from the first vocabulary is ambiguous, the receiver has two response actions: Firstly, she can randomly pick an object which is associated with the word as learned so far. Secondly, she can request a word from the sender's second vocabulary for the sender's referent. It is likely that the additional naming leads to an unequivocal identification of the object talked about. The utility function rewards successful identification. Thus, in all evolutionary simulations where the second vocabulary serves better than chance, requesting it (i.e., asking a wh-question) turns out to be the preferred strategy.

6 Conclusions and Future Work

We started the paper by reviewing a classic philosophical argument relating to normativity against basing semantics on sampling language use—a position embraced by distributional semantics. This argument is complemented by pointing out three classes of linguistic expressions which we suggested are intrinsically non-distributional. Making the case that meanings have to be learned in interactive language acquisition, both philosophical arguments as well as linguistic phenomena involving indexicals, proper names and wh-questions, suggest intrinsic problems for a semantics driven by the DH. Somewhat ironically, a construction plan appropriate for accounting for the linguistic phenomena under consideration can be found in the works of Firth in terms of 'contexts of situation'—although DS folklore hands Firth down exclusively as a founding figure of the distributional hypothesis. Accordingly, drawing on a semantic ontology of utterance situations, semantic objects and interactions, learning scenarios for indexicals, proper names and wh-questions are sketched that take Firth's notion of context seriously. While a semantics based on the DH suffers from shortcomings with respect to providing an adequate account of semantic learning, we conceptualise such an account by arguing for combining an ontology grounded in interaction with evolutionary game theory. To spell out the approach sketched here, future work needs to include running evolutionary simulation studies for those settings for which there is as yet no proof that they lead to lexical convergence.

We also identified a bootstrapping problem for DS that contributes to preventing it from being a self-supporting basis for semantics. But how does this assessment conform to the obvious success of DS in computational semantics? The reason, we think, is that a foundational semantics gives DS a piggyback: once there is independently justified meaning, usage regularities can be observed *post hoc*. We further hypothesise that this foundational semantics rests on interaction in context.

Acknowledgements

We acknowledge the support of the French Investissements d'Avenir-Labex EFL program (ANR-10-LABX-00). We also thank three reviewers for comments that helped to improve and clarify the arguments put forth in this paper.

References

Aina, L., C. Silberer, W. M. Sorodoc, Ionut-Teodor, and G. Boleda (2018). AMORE-UPF at SemEval-2018 task 4: BiLSTM with entity library. In *Proceedings of the 12th International Workshop on Semantic Evaluation*, SemEval-2018, Stroudsburg (PA), pp. 65–69. ACL.

Austin, J. L. (1950). Truth. In *Proceedings of the Aristotelian Society. Supplementary*, Volume xxiv, pp. 111–128. Reprinted in John L. Austin: *Philosophical Papers*. 2. ed. Oxford: Clarendon Press, 1970.

Baroni, M., R. Bernardi, and R. Zamparelli (2014). Frege in space: A program of compositional distributional semantics. *LiLT (Linguistic Issues in Language Technology) 9*.

Baroni, M. and A. Lenci (2010). Distributional memory: A general framework for corpus-based semantics. *Computational Linguistics 36*(4), 673–721.

Barwise, J. and J. Perry (1983). *Situations and Attitudes*. Stanford: CSLI Publications.

Boleda, G. and A. Herbelot (2016). Formal distributional semantics: Introduction to the special issue. *Computational Linguistics 42*(4), 619–635.

Bruni, E., N. K. Tran, and M. Baroni (2014). Multimodal distributional semantics. *Journal of Artificial Intelligence Research 49*, 1–47.

Chen, H. Y.-H. and J. D. Choi (2016). Character identification on multiparty conversation: Identifying mentions of characters in tv shows. In *Proceedings of the SIGDIAL 2016 Conference*, pp. 90–100.

Cooper, R. (2019). Type theory and language: From perception to linguistic communication. Book Draft.

Cooper, R., S. Dobnik, S. Larsson, and S. Lappin (2015). Probabilistic type theory and natural language semantics. *Linguistic Issues in Language Technology – LiLT 10*(4), 1–43.

De Vylder, B. and K. Tuyls (2006). How to reach linguistic consensus: A proof of convergence for the naming game. *Journal of Theoretical Biology 242*(4), 818–831.

Erk, K. (2016). What do you know about an alligator when you know the company it keeps? *Semantics and Pragmatics 9*(17), 1–63.

Firth, J. R. (1935). The technique of semantics. *Transactions of the Philological Society 34*(1), 36–73.

Firth, J. R. (1957). A synopsis of linguistic theory, 1930–1955. In *Studies in Linguistic Analysis* (Repr. 1962 ed.)., pp. 1–32. Oxford: Blackwell.

Ginzburg, J. (2012). *The Interactive Stance: Meaning for Conversation*. Oxford: Oxford University Press.

Ginzburg, J., R. Cooper, and T. Fernando (2014, April). Propositions, questions, and adjectives: a rich type theoretic approach. In *Proceedings of the EACL 2014 Workshop on Type Theory and Natural Language Semantics (TTNLS)*, Gothenburg, Sweden, pp. 89–96. Association for Computational Linguistics.

Gupta, A., G. Boleda, M. Baroni, and S. Padó (2015). Distributional vectors encode referential attributes. In *Proceedings of the 2015 Conference on Empirical Methods in Natural Language Processing*, EMNLP'15, pp. 12–21.

Harris, Z. (1954). Distributional structure. *Word 10*(23), 146–162.

Herbelot, A. (2015). Mr Darcy and Mr Toad, gentlemen: distributional names and their kinds. In *Proceedings of the 11th International Conference on Computational Semantics*, pp. 151–161.

Herbelot, A. and E. M. Vecchi (2015). Building a shared world: Mapping distributional to model-theoretic semantic spaces. In *Proceedings of the 2015 Conference on Empirical Methods in Natural Language Processing*, pp. 22–32.

Jäger, G. (2012). Game theory in semantics and pragmatics. In C. Maienborn, K. von Heusinger, and P. Portner (Eds.), *Semantics: an International Handbook of Natural Language Meaning*, Volume 3 of *Handbücher zur Sprach- und Kommunikationswissenschaft*, Chapter 4, pp. 2487–2516. De Gruyter Mouton.

Kripke, S. A. (1982). *Wittgenstein on Rules and Private Language: An Elementary Exposition*. Cambridge, MA: Harvard University Press.

Larsson, S. (2015). Formal semantics for perceptual classification. *Journal of Logic and Computation 25*(2), 335–369.

Lazaridou, A., A. Peysakhovich, and B. Marco (2017). In *Proceedings of the International Conference on Learning Representations*, ICLR 2017.

Lewis, D. (1969). *Convention: A Philosophical Study*. Cambridge, MA: Harvard University Press.

Lewis, D. (1970). General semantics. *Synthese 22*(1/2), 18–67.

Lücking, A. and A. Mehler (2012). What's the scope of the Naming Game? Constraints on semantic categorization. In *The Evolution of Language. Proceedings of the 9th International Conference*, Evolang IX, Kyoto, Japan, pp. 196–203.

McGinn, C. (1989). *Mental Content*. Oxford and New York: Basil Blackwell.

Millikan, R. G. (1984). *Language, Thought and Other Biological Categories*. Cambridge, MA: MIT Press.

Moradlou, S. and J. Ginzburg (2014). Learning to understand questions. In P. Muller and V. Rieser (Eds.), *Proceedings of SemDial 2014 (DialWatt)*, Heriot Watt University.

Moyer, M., K. Harrigan, V. Hacquard, and J. Lidz (2015). 2-year-olds' comprehension of personal pronouns. In E. Grillo, K. Jepson, and M. LaMendola (Eds.), *Boston University Conference on Language Development 39: Online Proceedings Supplement*, pp. 1–11. Boston Universtiy.

Mühlenbernd, R. and M. Franke (2012). Signaling conventions: Who learns what where and when in a social network? In *The Evolution of Language. Proceedings of the 9th International Conference*, Evolang IX, Kyoto, Japan, pp. 242–249.

Oshima-Takane, Y., Y. Takane, and T. R. Shultz (1999). The learning of first and second person pronouns in English: network models and analysis. *Journal of Child Language 26*(3), 545–575.

Sahlgren, M. (2005). An introduction to random indexing. `http://eprints.sics.se/221/1/RI_intro.pdf`.

Steels, L. (1997). The synthetic modeling of language origins. *Evolution of Communication 1*(1), 1–34.

Weston, J., S. Chopra, and A. Bordes (2014). Memory networks. `https://arxiv.org/abs/1410.3916`.

Towards Natural Language Story Understanding with Rich Logical Schemas

Lane Lawley and Gene Louis Kim and Lenhart Schubert
Department of Computer Science, University of Rochester
{llawley,gkim21,schubert}@cs.rochester.edu

Abstract

Generating "commonsense" knowledge for intelligent understanding and reasoning is a difficult, long-standing problem, whose scale challenges the capacity of any approach driven primarily by human input. Furthermore, approaches based on mining statistically repetitive patterns fail to produce the rich representations humans acquire, and fall far short of human efficiency in inducing knowledge from text. The idea of our approach to this problem is to provide a learning system with a "head start" consisting of a semantic parser, some basic ontological knowledge, and most importantly, a small set of very general schemas about the kinds of patterns of events (often purposive, causal, or socially conventional) that even a one- or two-year-old could reasonably be presumed to possess. We match these initial schemas to simple children's stories, obtaining concrete instances, and combining and abstracting these into new candidate schemas. Both the initial and generated schemas are specified using a rich, expressive logical form. Unlike the slot-and-filler structures often used in knowledge harvesting, this logical form allows us to specify complex relations and constraints over the slots. Though formal, the representations are language-like, and as such readily relatable to NL text. The agents, objects, and other roles in the schemas are represented by typed variables, and the event variables can be related through partial temporal ordering and causal relations. To match natural language stories with existing schemas, we first parse the stories into an underspecified variant of the logical form used by the schemas, which is suitable for most concrete stories. We include a walkthrough of matching a children's story to these schemas and generating inferences from these matches.

1 Introduction

Artificial general intelligence research tends to fall into one of two broad categories: connectionism, which emphasizes the importance of neural architectures in the human brain, and computationalism, which models human intelligence at a more abstract level, making use of knowledge representations and reasoning procedures. One common assumption in connectionist approaches is that an AI system can be trained from scratch, as a *tabula rasa*, once a suitable architecture has been specified. No representational or inferential mechanisms are presupposed—perhaps inevitably, because of the "black box" character of neural net functioning.

We believe that the need for exposure to massive amounts of sensory data can be averted with a suitable "head start". The basic knowledge representations, reasoning procedures, language abilities, and world knowledge of a 1- to 2-year-old human child must be attained in any general intelligence architecture, and we believe that learning from text, implemented atop a suitably powerful symbolic framework, will be easier than doing so using data-fitting methods alone.

Our approach is to generate knowledge in the form of abstract logical "schemas". Our system's "head start" includes a semantic parser, a general inference system over a highly expressive logical form, and an initial set of simple schemas that a very young child could plausibly possess. Our system parses natural language stories into a logical form, matches the story to existing schemas, draws inferences, and, upon recognition of patterns, generalizes new schemas, whose variable roles take the place of the individuals that vary from story to story.[1]

Schematic knowledge representations have a long history in artificial intelligence research; to underscore their usefulness, we will briefly outline that history and discuss some modern schema-oriented systems. We'll then describe our schema model in detail, differentiating it from past approaches, and describe its basic inference and generalization procedures, along with some examples of those procedures at work.

2 A Brief History of Schemas

The theoretical foundation of schemas has a history within cognitive science from even before AI existed as a field in order to explain the interactions of abstracted prior experience with language comprehension (Piaget, 1923; Bartlett, 1932; van Dijk and Kintsch, 1983). Cognitive science used schema-based theories to explain cognitive dissonance that occurs when faced with new information that cannot be accommodated by existing abstractions (Piaget and Inhelder, 1969), mistakes in memory surrounding schematic situations (Brewer and Treyens, 1981), and how we understand stories through an underlying grammar (Rumelhart, 1975). AI researchers with an eye for cognition computationalized these ideas into scripts and plans (Schank and Abelson, 1977) and frames (Minsky, 1975; Fillmore and Baker, 2010). Schank and Abelson's scripts successfully answered questions in the restaurant domain (among others) and Minsky's frames formed the basis for a number of AI systems for the remainder of the 20th century (Bobrow and Winograd, 1976; Fikes and Kehler, 1985; MacGregor and Burstein, 1991). However, these systems were limited to generating inferences from manually constructed frames.

Recent progress in learning schema-like knowledge has primarily been driven by applying statistical or neural network-based methods to large text corpora (Chambers and Jurafsky, 2011; Chambers, 2013; Pichotta and Mooney, 2016; Yuan et al., 2018). The learned schemas are quite limited in their capacity to enable inferences since they only describe high-level roles or temporal sequences. Perhaps this is all that can be expected from methods that are given minimal guidance and rely on many similar examples to find patterns. Wanzare et al. (2017) use crowdsourcing to help improve their clustering results and their scripts are made up of graph-ordered event clusters, but the clusters are groups of unstructured text segments. The goal of the schema framework we describe is to generate rich inferences which can be used to learn further schemas from a relatively limited number of examples.

3 Episodic Logic and Its Underspecified Form

Before diving into the details of our schemas, we first must describe the logical formalism in which the schemas are encoded, called Episodic Logic (EL) (Hwang, 1992; Hwang and Schubert, 1993; Schubert and Hwang, 2000). EL is a logical semantic representation that closely matches the form and expressive capacity of natural languages by extending FOL with semantic types and operators common in all languages. EL uses a small number type-shifting operators to map between specifically designated types to support the expressive power of natural language while keeping the underlying theoretical mechanisms simple. For example, EL uses reification operators to map predicate and sentence intensions to individuals. This allows predicate arguments in EL to denote both concrete and abstract entities (*Avicenna, the activity of writing poems, the idea that the universe revolves around the Earth*). Quantification remains first-order, with noun phrases treated as place-holders for constrained, quantified variables, in contrast with semantic theories that treat noun phrases as higher-order types. Another distinctive feature of EL, accounting for its name, is the *characterizing* operator. This operator, written $**$, relates an arbitrary EL formula to an episode it characterizes. If we restrict ourselves to positive, atomic predicates, $**$ closely resembles the Davidsonian use of event variables in predicates (Davidson, 1967). However, $**$ also allows complex characterizations of episodes, such as *Dana going hiking every weekend*, or *No nuclear nation being willing to eliminate its arsenal* (Schubert, 2000). An ontology of types is defined over the

[1]The code for our system is available at `https://github.com/bitbanger/schemas`.

Sentence *"Spot ran in the park"*

Episodic Logic	**Unscoped Logical Form**
`(some.d e: [e before.p |Now1|]`	`(|Spot| ((past run.v)`
`[[e in-loc.p |Park1|] ∧ [[|Spot| run1.v] ** e]]))`	`(adv-e (in.p (the.d park.n)))))`

Figure 1: EL and ULF formulas for an example sentence.

domain of individuals and includes categories such as basic individuals (e.g., *John, the Blarney Stone*, or *the Earth's magnetic field*), episodes (events, situations, processes), sets, numbers, propositions, and kinds. Schubert and Hwang (2000) provide a complete description of the ontology. EL has been shown to be suitable for deductive inference, uncertain inference, and Natural-Logic-like inference and has been used successfully to represent inference-enabling verb axioms (Morbini and Schubert, 2009; Schubert and Hwang, 2000; Schubert, 2014; Purtee and Schubert, 2017; Kim and Schubert, 2016). Inferences can be generated using the EPILOG inference engine (Morbini and Schubert, 2009; Schaeffer et al., 1993).

Most lexical items in EL are represented in the form `[word][sense num].[lexical type]`, e.g., `run1.v`.[2] Lexical types in EL are closely related to POS tags (e.g. `.v`, `.p`, and `.d` for verbs, prepositions, and determiners, respectively) but are constrained in their use by the EL semantic type system; e.g., modal *can* becomes `can.aux-s` or `can.aux-v` depending on its function as a sentence-level possibility operator or a VP-level ability operator. Names (denoting basic individuals) are represented by `|[name]|`, e.g. `|John|`. Predefined EL operators lack dot-extensions, e.g., `**`, `k`, `adv-a`. EL uses prefixed operators at the subsentential level (e.g., `(touch_down.v (on.p-arg |Mars|))`), and infix form at the sentence level (e.g., `[|InSight| (touch_down.v (on.p-arg |Mars|))]`). The distinction is emphasized in written EL by reserving square brackets for sentential formulas. Connectives allow for multiple arguments, i.e., `[w1 conn w2 ... wn]`, where the `wi` are sentential formulas and `conn` is `and` (∧) or `or` (∨). Quantification has a distinct syntax: `([determiner] [variable]: [restrictor] [nuclear scope])`. If omitted, the restrictor is implicitly True, thus allowing for FOL quantifiers ∀ and ∃.

Figure 1 shows an example of a complete EL formula and demonstrates how episode variables are used. The `**` operator characterizes an episode `e` (constrained by `[e before.p |Now1|]`) with the formula `[|Spot| run1.v]`, and the conjunct adds locative information about `e` derived from the `adv-e` modifier in the ULF version. Using the `**` operator, EL can characterize episodes with arbitrarily complex well-formed EL formulas.

Finally, here we introduce a few type shifting operators that appear in the schema examples. The kind forming operator, `k`, is a function from monadic nominal predicate intensions to kinds. The kind of action forming operator, `ka`, is a function from monadic verbal predicate intensions to kinds of actions.[3] The proposition forming operator, `that`, is a function from sentence intensions to propositions. Some examples (with tense suppressed):

"Gold is yellow" – `[(k gold.n) yellow.a]` *"Peter likes to run"* – `[|Peter| like.v (ka run.v)]`

"My dog believes that it is a wolf" – `(my.d x: [x dog.n] [x believe.v (that [x wolf.n])])`

3.1 Unscoped Logical Form

Unscoped (Episodic) Logical Form (ULF) is an underspecified variant of EL which models the formal types and predicate argument structure of EL while leaving anaphora, word sense, and operator scopes unresolved. It is the first step in the EL parsing process and captures the semantic and pragmatic signals that can be accessed from natural language syntax. Its proximity to syntax makes semantic parsing into ULF relatively simple while its commitment to EL types enables inferences that preserve semantic coherence within the logical formalism. It turns out that ULF provides enough semantic resolution for enabling schema inferences in most of the first-reader stories we have considered. For a small number of cases, the ambiguous components in ULFs are resolved on an as-needed basis. Here we describe ULF to the extent necessary to understand its application within the presented schema description and examples.

[2]We use WordNet senses in this document (Miller, 1995), but EL is not strictly tied to WordNet.

[3]`ka` can be expressed in terms of `k`, forming a kind whose instances are agent-event pairs.

Kim and Schubert (2019) provides a more complete description of ULF and its uses outside of schemas.

Figure 1 shows the ULF for a sentence alongside the EL interpretation and demonstrates a few key differences between EL and ULF.

1. **ULF does not have episode variables.** ULF preserves type coherence in the face of implicit episodes and actions by introducing operators to form episode- and action-modifying adverbials from predicate intensions (`adv-e`, `adv-a`). Tense and aspectual operators are also implicitly episode-modifiers.
2. **Scope, anaphora, and word sense are unresolved.** Without scope or anaphora resolution, *"the park"* is simply `(the.d park.n)` in ULF compared to the referentially resolved `|Park1|` (or a Skolem constant if unresolvable) in EL. Without word senses, the lexical items are represented as `[word].[lexical tag]`.
3. **ULF only uses parentheses for bracketing.** The operator position is inferred from the semantic types of the bracketed elements.

4 Schema Form and Meaning

We will refer to the example schema in Figure 2—the generic schema for one agent giving an object to another agent for possession—as we explain the form and meaning of our schemas. This is one of our system's initial schemas. It is particularly simple, even in terms of the initial schemas we are assuming, in that it contains just a single "step". Such single-step schemas can specialize the type of action represented by the single step, or even just supply type information, preconditions, and effects, without specializing the step-concept.

```
(epi-schema
  ((?x give_obj_for_poss.v ?y ?o) ** ?e)
  (:Nonfluent-conds
    !r1 (?x agent.n)
    !r2 (?y agent.n)
    !r3 (?o object.n)
    !r4 (?l location.n) )

  (:Init-conds
    ?i1 (?x (can.aux-v (give_to.v ?y ?o)))
    ?i2 (?x (be.v (adv-e (at.p ?l))))
    ?i3 (?y (be.v (adv-e (at.p ?l)))) )

  (:Goals
    ?g1 (?x want.v
      (that (?y (have.v ?o)))) )

  (:Steps
    ?e1 (?x (give_to.v ?y ?o)) )

  (:Post-conds
    ?p1 (?y (possess.v ?o)) )

  (:Episode-relations
    !w1 (?e1 same-time ?e)
    !w2 (?e1 consec ?p1)
    !w3 (?e1 cause-of.n ?p1) ) )
```

Figure 2: An example schema.

4.1 Overall Structure

A schema comprises a schema type and header, shown here in the first line of the schema, followed by a list of sections. Sections are lists of logical formulas, indexed by a unique (across all sections) identifier, and fall into one of two types: *episode sections*, in which all identifiers begin with a question mark (*?*), and *nonfluent sections*, in which all identifiers begin with an exclamation mark (*!*). Each *?*-identifier in an episode section introduces an episode characterized by the formula that follows.

4.2 Episode vs. Nonfluent Sections

Fluent conditions, or episodic conditions, are "susceptible to change" over time. Nonfluent conditions hold true regardless of time. We specify nonfluent conditions in sections whose identifiers begin with (*!*). Within nonfluent sections, such as `:Nonfluent-conds` or `:Episode-relations`, we interpret any non-fluent condition identifier $\texttt{!nf}_N$ as an alias (metavariable) that can be freely substituted for its associated formula Φ_N. Within episode sections, such as `:Steps` or `:Init-conds`, we interpret any episode condition identifier $\texttt{?e}_N$ as an episode variable that is characterized by its associated formula Ψ_N.

4.3 Initial and Post Conditions

Initial conditions are a form of fluent predication—they must be true at the outset of the schema, but might not be true for the entire schema episode. They might be true before the start of the schema, or they might become true at the exact start time of the schema. This temporal relationship is encoded, for each initial condition episode `?i`$_N$, by the tacit assumption of the nonfluent episode-relational predication `((start-of.f ?e) during ?i`$_N$`)`. Postconditions may be true at any time, but must be true at least at the end point of the schema, or immediately afterward, so for each postcondition episode `?p`$_N$, we tacitly assume the nonfluent predication `((end-of.f ?e) during ?p`$_N$`)`.

4.4 Header

The schema in Figure 2 is an *epi-schema*, that is, an *episodic* schema. It describes an episode in the episodic logic sense. The episode it describes, here `?e`, is called the "head episode" of the schema. The header provides a characterizing formula of the head episode. Derivation of the header characterization from a story sentence, here `give_obj_for_poss.v`, certainly implies the rest of the schema, but that is not necessarily true in the reverse direction (see Section 5.1 for a note on "confirming" schemas). An epi-schema can be viewed as defining an episode type (at least partially), where all *?*-variables in the header and body of a schema, except the head episode, are Skolem functions (equivalently, role functions) of that episode. As such, they can be equated to externally supplied constants. For example, the location variable `?l` in Figure 2 is interpreted as a Skolem function of `?e`, so that if `?e` receives a particular value, say `|EP1|`, then `(?l |EP1|)` in effect denotes the location of the participants; this might become equated to an external constant such as `|Home23|`.

4.5 Steps and Goals

The steps section enumerates the episodes that occur in, and constitute, the head episode, and their order of enumeration here sets the default event ordering. Goals are also episodes within the schema, but underlining their teleological contribution is necessary for action understanding, planning, and meta-reasoning—people do things for reasons.

4.6 Episode Relations

The episode relations section specifies temporal and causal constraints on the subepisodes belonging to the schema episode, including overriding the default relations for `:Init-conds` and `:Steps`. In Figure 2, episode `?e1` is characterized by some agent `?x` giving some object `?o` to some agent `?y`. A postcondition episode, `?p1`, is characterized by `?y` having that object. The episode relation section says that `?e1` and `?p1` are consecutive, and further that `?e1` is the direct cause of `?p1`. Temporal constraints in this section—which can relate the start times and end times of episodes, or provide uncertainty about start or end times—can induce a directed acyclic graph (DAG) of start and end times, a full interval graph, or a causality graph for action planning. Even the simplest induced graph, the DAG of start times, helps us to rule out schemas whose events are temporally inconsistent with a story. In the example schema, the constraint `!w1` says that step episode `?e1` shares a start and end time (a.k.a. `same-time`) with the schema's head episode `?e`. We intend `give_to.v` to generalize `give_obj_for_poss.v`. Under certain assumptions about event individuation (Schubert, 2000), this generalization relation together with the `same-time` predication actually implies that `(?e1 = ?e)`; so finding a story assertion matching `(?x give_to.v ?y ?o)` would suggest that the instantiation attempt for the schema is "on the right track".

5 Schema Matching and Inferences

Using schemas to make sense of a story requires casting the story in terms of schemas: We must find "matches" between sentences and individuals in the story, and formulas and roles in the schema. We have designed, implemented, and experimented with a basic algorithm which takes a ULF parse of a story, performs some preprocessing to get a basic EL form, matches the formulas in the story to new schemas as well as schema instances stored in "working memory", generates inferences from those schemas after filling in their variables, and uses those inferences to fill in yet more schemas. In this section, we detail the algorithm, and walk through an example from one of our experiments on a children's first reader story from *The New McGuffey First Reader* (McGuffey, 1901).

5.1 Matching Algorithm

Algorithm 1 Algorithm for matching story formulas to schemas

```
INPUT: set of story episodes ST
MODIFIES: knowledge base of facts KB
KB ← ∅
for story episode E in ST do
  for conjunctive sub-formula F in E do
    KB ← KB ∪ {F}
  while ∃ unprocessed formula F_ST ∈ KB do
    for episode E_SCH in SCH episodes (linearized timeline) do
      for formula F_SCH ∈ E_SCH do
        MGU ← most general unifier of F_SCH and F_ST
        if MGU does not exist then
          continue
        for variable binding B = V_SCH → T_ST do
          if V_SCH is not already bound to something else then
            substitute T_ST for all occurrences of V_SCH in the schema instance
        if schema instance is confirmed then
          for fully-bound formula F_B in the instance do
            KB ← KB ∪ {F_B}
    mark F_ST as processed
```

The matching algorithm takes a (potentially partially-filled) schema instance *SCH*, which is a schema and a map of its bound variable names to their values, and a story *ST*, which is a list of episodes, with their characterizing formulas, along with type predications, etc. Each step to match a story WFF is based on a global "knowledge base" of episodes and formulas we know to be true. The knowledge base is initialized with the story WFF, and the schema instantiation process then begins. We can create a new schema instance, or update an existing one, when a WFF in the knowledge base "matches" a WFF in the schema, i.e., is successfully unified. We obtain the "most general unifier" (MGU) using the algorithm by Robinson (1965). The MGU acts as a variable-to-term mapping, which we then use to replace variables throughout the schema instance. If a schema instance is "confirmed", we "infer" formulas within the schema whose variables have all been made concrete, and we add them to the knowledge base. As our initial schemas are quite simple, our current confirmation heuristic is simply whether all episodes in the `:Steps` section have been matched. As we continue to develop with more complex stories, and as schemas grow more complex, a more nuanced approach—perhaps involving certainties and numbers of variables mapped—is called for. Once the knowledge base has been updated, we return back to the schema matching step; we stop when we can no longer instantiate new schemas, or update existing instances, and move on to the next story WFF.

5.2 Planning and Meta-Reasoning

As the reasoning procedures and initial schemas are hypothesized to be quite general, we can make inferences about the beliefs and desires of agents within the story by "simulating" their reasoning with our own algorithms. A simple example of such an inference is that, if a mother wants her daughter to have a cat, and we know, via our general schemas, that owning a cat is pleasurable, we infer that the mother knew that her daughter having a cat would cause her daughter to experience pleasure, and we infer that the mother wanted her daughter to experience pleasure. We can draw many parallels to the

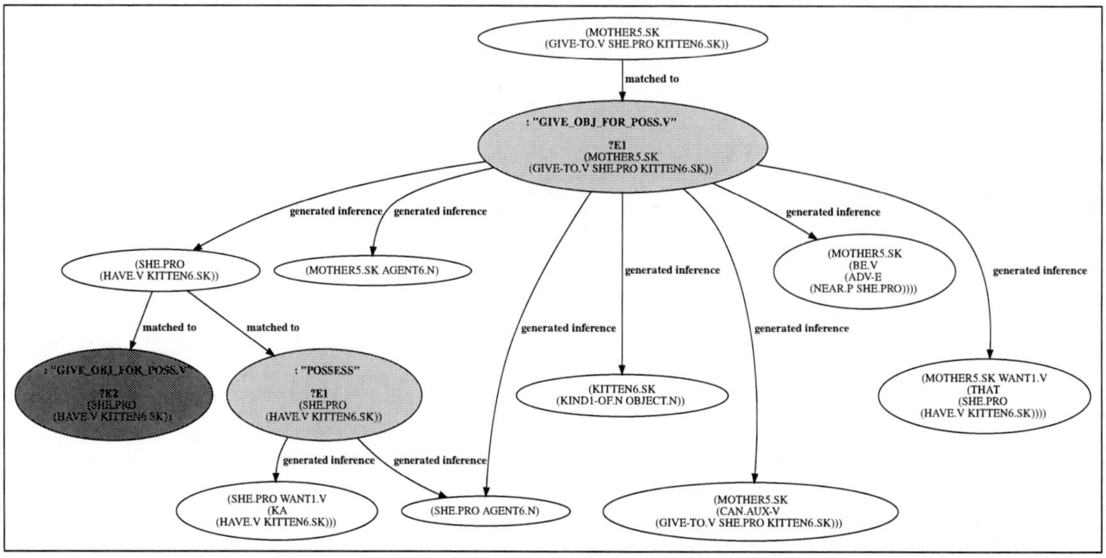

Figure 3: A graph of inferences made while processing a single story sentence. White vertices are inferred and story WFFs, green bubbles are "confirmed" schemas (see Section 5.1 for definition), and red bubbles are unconfirmed schemas.

planning domain: As agents have desires and beliefs, and schemas have goals, preconditions, and side effects, one could use existing schemas to solve planning problems, and, in turn, use planning algorithms to hypothesize new schemas for accomplishing certain goals.

5.3 Matching Example

Starting with the story sentence "Her mother gave the kitten to her" parsed into its EL form `(MOTHER5.SK (GIVE_TO.V SHE.PRO KITTEN6.SK))`, we'll walk through the matching algorithm, whose generated inferences are shown in Figure 3.

5.3.1 ULF Processing

We first process the ULF verb predication `((past give.v) (the.d kitten.n) (to.p-arg her.pro))` in Figure 4 to attach the argument marking preposition to the verb and float its argument to the front of the list. We then Skolemize the `the.d` determiners, demoting the relational noun predicate `(mother-of.n she.pro)` to the bare noun predicate `mother.n` to derive the Skolem name `MOTHER5.SK` (the 5 is a cumulative counter for Skolem constants; it is arbitrary, and an artifact of our Skolemization process), and using the noun predicate `kitten.n` to derive the Skolem name `KITTEN6.SK`. We finally obtain the EL sentence `(MOTHER5.SK (GIVE_TO.V SHE.PRO KITTEN6.SK))`, which is ready for matching.

5.3.2 The Initial Match

`GIVE_TO.V` immediately matches to the schema shown in Figure 2, as that schema has the same name. We unify the story formula `(MOTHER5.SK (GIVE_TO.V SHE.PRO KITTEN6.SK))` with the schema header, producing the unifier (`?x` ← `MOTHER5.SK`, `?y` ← `SHE.PRO`, `?o` ← `KITTEN6.SK`), and we then make that substitution throughout the entire schema. Notably, every role in the schema is now bound except for the location `?l`. Note that, although the question of whether a schema is "confirmed" to have happened at any point in the matching process is difficult to answer in general, it is easy here: The actual verb in the schema's single step has been observed, so in the absence of type conflicts it is quite likely that the rest of the schema happened. All of the filled-in WFFs in the `Events`, `Goals`, `Init-conds`, and `Nonfluent-conds` sections, except those including the still-unbound variable `?l`, are added to our knowledge base as inferences from a confirmed schema.

```
; Here is May with her kitten.
(|May| ((pres be.v) here.a
       (adv-a (with.p (the.d (λx ((x kitten.n) and.cc (x (poss-by her.pro)))))))))
; Her mother gave the kitten to her.
((the.d (mother-of.n her.pro)) ((past give.v) (the.d kitten.n) (to.p-arg she.pro)))
; She is kind to the pretty kitten.
(she.pro ((pres be.v) kind.a
          (adv-a (to.p (the.d (pretty.a kitten.n))))))
; She likes to see it jump and play.
(she.pro ((pres like.v) (ka (see it.v (jump.v and.cc play.v)))))
; See it run with May's ball!
(({you}.pro ((pres see.v) it.pro
    (run.v (adv-a (with.d (the.d (λ x ((x ball.n) and.cc (x (poss-by |May|)))))))))) !)
; It does not run far with it.
(it.pro ((pres do.aux-s) not
         (run.v far.adv-a (adv-a (with.p it.pro)))))
; If May can get the ball she will not take it.
((if.ps (|May| ((pres can.aux-v) (get.v (the.d ball.n)))))
 (she.pro ((pres will.aux-s) not (take.v it.pro))))
; She will give it to the kitten to play with.
(she.pro ((pres will.aux-s)
          (give.v (to.p-arg (the.d kitten.n)) it.pro
           (adv-a ({for}.p (ka (play-with.v {it}.pro)))))))
```

Figure 4: A children's story, in partially post-processed ULF form. These were manually annotated but there are promising preliminary results on parsing ULF (Kim, 2019)

5.3.3 Further Matching

While the story sentence has now been matched, it has generated inferences, and those inferences might match other schemas. So, we are not done; we must attempt to match each of those before moving on to the next story sentence. Indeed, in this case, the inference (SHE.PRO (HAVE.V KITTEN6.SK)) matches to two schemas: GIVE_TO.v and POSSESS.V; the former is unconfirmed (but, upon close inspection, would appear to be an incomplete copy of the instance that generated its matched WFF), and the latter was triggered (and confirmed) by the HAVE.V verb predicate in the inference. The POSSESS.V schema generates two more inferences, one of which was also generated by the original GIVE_TO.V schema, and the matching process concludes for this sentence, as all generated inferences have been matched to all possible schemas.

6 Conclusion & Future Work

Our approach to schemas comprises a rich logical language, initial schemas providing "low-level" inferences about the effects and motivations behind simple, general actions, and a way of doing "fuzzy matching" of inexact, but similar, formulas (see Section 6.2). All of these components work together to provide inferences that enable a comprehensive, structured, and human-oriented "fleshing out" of events in stories. The inferences we generate can then be combined, generalized, and reasoned about, thus creating new schemas from relatively few examples. There is much work remaining to further develop our parsing, matching, and especially our generalization processes. We proceed here to outline some of that future work—our initial results from matching a small handful of initial schemas to a short children's story are promising.

6.1 Immediate Future: Generalization

Currently, we are focusing our efforts on the task of schema generalization: Given two (or more) sequences of predications, which may themselves contain nested schemas, can we create a schema that describes both stories with a more general pattern? We are currently experimenting on four short children's stories about fishing, and each story includes similar words used in similar contexts: "These men fish in the sea", "We will take the long rod, and the hook and line", "Here is Tom with his rod and line", "Sometimes they sit on the bank of the river", and many more thematically parallel sentences in the stories strongly suggest a schema where people are near water, have a rod, and catch fish with a rod or a net. After extracting a set of recurring events from the stories—like going to water, having a rod, catching fish, and putting fish in a basket—we plan to experiment with using narrative models like tense trees (Hwang and Schubert, 1992) to find subsequences of the events that could be interpreted as steps in a schema.

After extracting subsequences of similar events that occur in two or more stories, we can use knowledge of basic motivations—e.g. people often want to possess things—to infer a teleology of those events. If some unknown action "catch ?x" always occurs before "possess ?x", we might hypothesize that the catching something has an effect of possessing that thing. If that sequence is only ever seen with fish and crabs as ?x, our confidence in the "catch to possess" schema might be lower when the object is not a marine animal, implying a "catch marine animal to possess" schema. Teleological inferences will likely prove to be very useful in sifting out reasonable new schema generalizations from a large collection of partly nonsensical ones.

Generalization can also take place from *one* example: after matching certain individual constants from a story to slots in a schema, we can consult a generalization hierarchy for those individuals' types (e.g. dog -> canine -> animal -> object), and select appropriate generalizations for the slots. These selections do not necessarily need to be made right away: the entire generalization hierarchy can be stored, and usage frequencies can be accumulated when more examples are found. However, they also do allow immediate generalization: a "reasonable guess" could be provided by the generalized word that's used the most frequently in some text corpus, for example. Further, if conditions are imposed on the entity by other formulas in the schema, the most general word that still satisfies those conditions could be selected, similar to the schema generalization in the GENESIS system (Mooney, 1990). For example, "border collie" could be replaced with "dog" if there were a later assertion that "the border collie competed in a dog show", but replacing it with "animal" would be too general.

6.2 "Fuzzy Matching"

So far, we have mostly discussed exact matching of WFFs using the MGU algorithm. However, in many cases, we will want to match something like a "Segway" to a schema predication about a "vehicle", just as readily as we would match "car" to "vehicle". Additionally, synonyms and intuitively similar words, like "run" and "jog", should be able to match as well, perhaps with some certainty score. Hypernym hierarchies, semantic word embeddings, and logical world knowledge of object properties all affect whether we want to make inexact matches. We are actively researching how best to gather and use this information in the matching process—as well as how to index schemas for quick retrieval, even when matches are inexact.

6.3 A Note on Condition Strictness

It is currently unclear exactly how and when condition violations are acceptable. Certainly, to generalize new schemas, we must allow some "slack" in condition violations: a schema that fits, say, a "fishing" schema perfectly, except the variable constrained to be a fish is actually a crab, should cause us to infer that "catching seafood" might be a good generalization to store. However, different conditions intuitively seem violable to different degrees, and in different contexts, depending on what other conditions are met or violated. Many factors seem to affect whether we match or abandon a schema, or create a new schema, when trying to make sense of a story. These factors will be the subject of many future experiments.

6.4 Scaling the Matching Algorithm

Our algorithm is in an early stage, and several scaling problems must be solved to bring it to bear on an unsupervised learning task. We are currently experimenting on an assortment of children's first reader stories to determine rules and heuristics to guide us as we develop the matching algorithm to cope with large numbers of possible schema matches.

6.4.1 Role Assignment Restriction

As the number of schemas scales, it will be combinatorially infeasible to maintain every possible schema instance a story WFF might prompt; if there are three humans in a schema, and ten humans mentioned in a story, there are $\binom{10}{3}$ ways to instantiate the human roles alone in that schema. In many cases, it may suffice to "let the actions speak for the agents", that is, prefer to use verb predications to identify individuals for schema roles, rather than considering role assignments directly. The schema relates arguments to its verb predications to their role definitions and "type" predications, so if we can infer that `?x` is `|Mary|` from an action that she did, we can then simply confirm or refute the additional constraint `(?x human.n)`. However, there could be examples where there is still suitable ambiguity, or where "action-first" role assignment isn't the most efficient; we hope to discover and address these examples in our ongoing story experiments.

6.4.2 Instance Abandonment

What might seem like a "promising" schema match at first could diverge suitably from the story and become useless; we would want to abandon it to free up memory, and so we don't continue fruitless comparisons of story WFFs to it. However, it is difficult to know when a schema instance is unlikely to continue to be matched to WFFs; sentences read, or inferences generated, much later on in a story could provide the missing piece to a schema instance matched many sentences ago. We plan to use our ongoing story experiments to formulate abandonment heuristics as well, or even identify potential applications of machine learning to the problem.

6.4.3 Schema Retrieval

As the number of schemas grows, and as we allow for inexact matching, whether of hypernyms, synonyms, or "functionally equivalent" terms (based on world knowledge), the task of identifying reasonable schemas as match candidates grows more difficult in turn. As a first step, indexing schemas by a handful of specific predications—specific verbs and nouns, chosen to maximally prune the search space—could allow for quick identification of relevant schemas. From there, indexing by sequences, or subsequences, of events should help us quickly identify highly specific sequential schemas within a large corpus; the human brain seems to be able to recall schemas very quickly with very terse sequences, as Winograd (1973) demonstrates with the sequence "skid, crash, hospital". Finally, any indexing we've done will need to be augmented to perform well even with inexact matching as described above. Schema retrieval optimization will be heavily informed by our experiments with the matching space on real stories, and especially as our number of schemas grows.

7 Acknowledgements

We would like to thank Benjamin Kane, Benjamin Kuehnert, Sophie Sackstein, and Georgiy Platonov for their development assistance and participation in schema-related discussions. This work was supported by the NSF NRT Fellowship DGE-1449828, and DARPA CwC subcontract W911NF-15-1-0542.

References

Bartlett, F. C. (1932). *Remembering: A Study in Experimental and Social Psychology.* Cambridge University Press.

Bobrow, D. G. and T. Winograd (1976). On overview of KRL, a knowledge representation language. *Cognitive Science 1*, 3–46.

Brewer, W. F. and J. C. Treyens (1981). Role of schemata in memory for places. *Cognitive Psychology 13*(2), 207–230.

Chambers, N. (2013). Event schema induction with a probabilistic entity-driven model. In *Proceedings of the 2013 Conference on Empirical Methods in Natural Language Processing*, pp. 1797–1807. Association for Computational Linguistics.

Chambers, N. and D. Jurafsky (2011). Template-based information extraction without the templates. In *Proceedings of the 49th Annual Meeting of the Association for Computational Linguistics: Human Language Technologies*, pp. 976–986. Association for Computational Linguistics.

Davidson, D. (1967). The logical form of action sentences. In N. Rescher (Ed.), *The Logic of Decision and Action*. University of Pittsburgh Press.

Fikes, R. and T. Kehler (1985, September). The role of frame-based representation in reasoning. *Commun. ACM 28*(9), 904–920.

Fillmore, C. J. and C. Baker (2010). A frames approach to semantic analysis. In B. Heine and H. Narrog (Eds.), *The Oxford handbook of linguistic analysis*, pp. 313–340. Oxford University Press.

Hwang, C. and L. Schubert (1993). Episodic Logic: A situational logic for natural language processing. In P. Aczel, D. Israel, Y. Katagiri, and S. Peters (Eds.), *Situation Theory and its Applications 3 (STA-3)*, pp. 307–452. CSLI.

Hwang, C. H. (1992). *A logical approach to narrative understanding*. Ph. D. thesis, University of Alberta.

Hwang, C. H. and L. K. Schubert (1992). Tense trees as the "fine structure" of discourse. In *Proceedings of the 30th Annual Meeting on Association for Computational Linguistics*, ACL '92, Stroudsburg, PA, USA, pp. 232–240. Association for Computational Linguistics.

Kim, G. and L. Schubert (2016, August). High-fidelity lexical axiom construction from verb glosses. In *Proceedings of the Fifth Joint Conference on Lexical and Computational Semantics*, Berlin, Germany, pp. 34–44. Association for Computational Linguistics.

Kim, G. and L. Schubert (2019, May). A type-coherent, expressive representation as an initial step to language understanding. In *Proceedings of the 13th International Conference on Computational Semantics*, Gothenburg, Sweden. Association for Computational Linguistics.

Kim, G. L. (2019). Towards parsing unscoped episodic logical forms with a cache transition parser. In *the Poster Abstracts of the Proceedings of the 32nd International Conference of the Florida Artificial Intelligence Research Society*.

MacGregor, R. M. and M. H. Burstein (1991). Using a description classifier to enhance knowledge representation. *IEEE Expert 6*, 41–46.

McGuffey, W. H. (1901). *The New McGuffey First Reader*. American Book Company.

Miller, G. A. (1995, November). WordNet: A lexical database for english. *Communications of the ACM 38*(11), 39–41.

Minsky, M. (1975). A framework for representing knowledge. In P. H. Winston (Ed.), *The psychology of computer vision*. Cambridge, Massachusetts: McGraw-Hill.

Mooney, R. J. (1990). *A general explanation-based learning mechanism and its application to narrative understanding.* Morgan Kaufmann.

Morbini, F. and L. Schubert (2009, June). Evaluation of Epilog: A reasoner for Episodic Logic. In *Proceedings of the Ninth International Symposium on Logical Formalizations of Commonsense Reasoning*, Toronto, Canada.

Piaget, J. (1923). *Langage et pensée chez l'enfant (The Language and Thought of the Child).* Neuchâtel: Delachaux et Niestlé.

Piaget, J. and B. Inhelder (1969). *The Psychology of the Child.* New York: Basic Books.

Pichotta, K. and R. Mooney (2016). Statistical script learning with recurrent neural networks. In *Proceedings of the Workshop on Uphill Battles in Language Processing: Scaling Early Achievements to Robust Methods*, pp. 11–16. Association for Computational Linguistics.

Purtee, A. and L. Schubert (2017). Simple rules for probabilistic commonsense reasoning. In *Proceedings of the 5th Ann. Conf. on Advances in Cognitive Systems (ACS 2017).* Cognitive Systems Foundation.

Robinson, J. A. (1965). A machine-oriented logic based on the resolution principle. *Journal of the ACM 12*(1), 23–41.

Rumelhart, D. E. (1975). Notes on a schema for stories. In D. G. BOBROW and A. COLLINS (Eds.), *Representation and Understanding*, pp. 211–236. San Diego: Morgan Kaufmann.

Schaeffer, S., C. Hwang, J. de Haan, and L. Schubert (1993). EPILOG, the computational system for episodic logic: User's guide. Technical report, Department of Computer Science, University of Alberta.

Schank, R. C. and R. P. Abelson (1977). *Scripts, plans, goals and understanding: An inquiry into human knowledge structures.* Oxford, England: Lawrence Erlbaum.

Schubert, L. (2014, June). From treebank parses to Episodic Logic and commonsense inference. In *Proceedings of the ACL 2014 Workshop on Semantic Parsing*, Baltimore, MD, pp. 55–60. Association for Computational Linguistics.

Schubert, L. K. (2000). The situations we talk about. In J. Minker (Ed.), *Logic-based Artificial Intelligence*, pp. 407–439. Norwell, MA, USA: Kluwer Academic Publishers.

Schubert, L. K. and C. H. Hwang (2000). Episodic Logic meets Little Red Riding Hood: A comprehensive natural representation for language understanding. In L. M. Iwańska and S. C. Shapiro (Eds.), *Natural Language Processing and Knowledge Representation*, pp. 111–174. Cambridge, MA, USA: MIT Press.

van Dijk, T. A. and W. Kintsch (1983). *Strategies of Discourse Comprehension.* New York: Academic Press.

Wanzare, L., A. Zarcone, S. Thater, and M. Pinkal (2017). Inducing script structure from crowdsourced event descriptions via semi-supervised clustering. In *Proceedings of the 2nd Workshop on Linking Models of Lexical, Sentential and Discourse-level Semantics*, pp. 1–11. Association for Computational Linguistics.

Winograd, T. (1973). A procedural model of language understanding. In R. Schank and K. Colby (Eds.), *Computer Models of Thought and Language*, pp. 152–186. New York, NY: WH Freeman.

Yuan, Q., X. Ren, W. He, C. Zhang, X. Geng, L. Huang, H. Ji, C.-Y. Lin, and J. Han (2018). Open-schema event profiling for massive news corpora. In *Proceedings of the 27th ACM International Conference on Information and Knowledge Management*, CIKM '18, New York, NY, USA, pp. 587–596. ACM.

Questions in Dependent Type Semantics

Kazuki Watanabe
The University of Tokyo
watanabe-kazuki163@g.ecc.u-tokyo.ac.jp

Koji Mineshima
Ochanomizu University
mineshima.koji@ocha.ac.jp

Daisuke Bekki
Ochanomizu University
bekki@is.ocha.ac.jp

1 Introduction

Dependent Type Semantics (DTS; Bekki and Mineshima (2017)) is a semantic framework that provides a unified analysis of presupposition and anaphora, based on dependent type theory (Martin-Löf, 1984). The semantic representations for declarative sentences in DTS are *types*, based on the propositions-as-types paradigm. While type-theoretic semantics for natural language based on dependent type theory has been developed (Ranta, 1994; Luo, 2012; Cooper, 2012; Chatzikyriakidis and Luo, 2017, among others), how to assign semantic representations to *interrogative* sentences in such a framework has been a non-trivial problem. In this study, we show how to provide the semantics of interrogative sentences in DTS. The basic idea is to assign the same type to both declarative sentences and interrogative sentences, partly building on the recent proposal in Inquisitive Semantics (Ciardelli et al., 2019), where interrogative and declarative sentences are treated as having the same type.

While our extension of DTS adopts some notions from Inquisitive Semantics, there is a difference between the two approaches. Crucially, while double negation is a key to make a distinction between assertion and question in Inquisitive Semantics, we do not make use of double negation for this purpose because it blocks anaphoric links in terms of Σ-types in DTS (see section 3.4 for the detail).

Another difference is that DTS is based on the idea of proof-theoretic semantics where the meaning of a sentence is given in terms of inference rules. The proof-theoretic approach is particularly suited for computational approaches to semantics and natural language inference; we use Combinatory Categorial Grammar (CCG; Steedman (1996)) as a syntactic component of DTS and implement our compositional semantics for interrogative sentences using ccg2lambda[1] (Martínez-Gómez et al., 2016), a semantic parsing platform based on CCG. Also, on the basis of the idea that the relationship between a question and an answer can be formulated as a task of Recognizing Textual Entailment (RTE), we implement our inference system using proof assistant Coq (The Coq Development Team, 2016)[2] and show that our system can deal with a wide range of question-answer relationships.[3] For this purpose, we build a testset to evaluate interrogative semantics and inference system, which consists of 49 question-answer pairs discussed in the formal semantics literature. Using proof automation in Coq, we implement a proof system for DTS that can prove these question-answer relationships formulated as RTE problems.

In short, the contributions of this research are threefold: (i) to present a compositional semantics in DTS for various types of questions, including polar questions, alternative questions, and wh-questions; (ii) to implement our compositional semantics and proof system to solve question answering as RTE problem; and (iii) to create a testset compiling question-answer pairs discussed in the literature and evaluate our implemented system on it.

[1] `https://github.com/mynlp/ccg2lambda`

[2] See Chatzikyriakidis and Luo (2014) for the use of Coq in formalizing natural language inferences in dependent type theory.

[3] The system will be available at `https://github.com/Kazuuuuuki/DTS-question-parser`.

$$\frac{\begin{array}{cc} & \overline{x:A}^{\,k} \\ & \vdots \\ A : type_i & B : type_j \end{array}}{(x:A) \to B : type_{max(i,j)}} \ (\Pi F), k \qquad \frac{\begin{array}{cc} & \overline{x:A}^{\,k} \\ & \vdots \\ A : type_i & M : B \end{array}}{\lambda x.M : (x:A) \to B} \ (\Pi I), k \qquad \frac{M : (x:A) \to B \quad N : A}{MN : B[N/x]} \ (\Pi E)$$

$$\frac{\begin{array}{cc} & \overline{x:A}^{\,k} \\ & \vdots \\ A : type_i & B : type_j \end{array}}{\begin{bmatrix} x:A \\ B \end{bmatrix} : type_{max(i,j)}} \ (\Sigma F), k \qquad \frac{M : A \quad N : B[M/x]}{(M,N) : \begin{bmatrix} x:A \\ B \end{bmatrix}} \ (\Sigma I) \qquad \frac{M : \begin{bmatrix} x:A \\ B \end{bmatrix}}{\pi_1(M) : A} \ (\Sigma E) \qquad \frac{M : \begin{bmatrix} x:A \\ B \end{bmatrix}}{\pi_2(M) : B[\pi_1(M)/x]} \ (\Sigma E)$$

$$\frac{A : type_i \quad B : type_j}{A \uplus B : type_{max(i,j)}} \ (\uplus F) \qquad \frac{M : A}{\iota_1(M) : A \uplus B} \ (\uplus I) \qquad \frac{M : B}{\iota_2(M) : A \uplus B} \ (\uplus I)$$

$$\frac{\begin{array}{cccc} & & \overline{x:A}^{\,k} & \overline{x:B}^{\,k} \\ & & \vdots & \vdots \\ L : A \uplus B & C : (A \uplus B) \to type_i & M : C(\iota_1(x)) & N : C(\iota_2(x)) \end{array}}{case\ L\ of\ (\lambda x.M; \lambda x.N) : C(L)} \ (\uplus E), k$$

$$\frac{}{\{a_1, \ldots, a_n\} : type_i} \ (\{\}\ \mathrm{F}) \qquad \frac{}{a_k : \{a_1, \ldots, a_n\}} \ (\{\}\ \mathrm{I})$$

$$\frac{M : \{a_1, \ldots, a_n\} \quad C : \{a_1, \ldots, a_n\} \to type_i \quad N_1 : C(a_1) \quad \ldots \quad N_n : C(a_n)}{case_M(N_1, \ldots, N_n) : C(M)} \ \{\}\ \mathrm{E}$$

Figure 1: Inference rules

There exist other semantic frameworks based on dependent type theory which deal with interrogative sentences. Ginzburg (2005) assigns different types to declarative sentences (assertion) and interrogative sentences (question); assertion is assigned a record type, while question is assigned the type of functions that maps records to propositions. In Ranta (1994), some meta-rules are introduced for describing the relationship of answers to the corresponding questions. A detailed comparison between our framework and these other type-theoretic frameworks must be left for another occasion.

The structure of the paper is as follows. In section 2 we briefly introduce the framework of DTS (for more detail, see Bekki (2014); Bekki and Mineshima (2017); Tanaka et al. (2018)). The main part of this paper is section 3. In this section, we extend the basic theory of DTS and present semantic representations for basic interrogative sentences. We show that this extension preserves the analysis of anaphora in terms of Σ-types in DTS. In section 4, we give an overview of how to provide a compositional semantics to derive semantic representations using CCG as a syntactic framework. In section 5, we present a question-answering testset for evaluating interrogative semantics and the evaluation of our system on the testset. In section 6, we briefly discuss some future work.

2 DTS

In this section, we explain a basic framework of DTS that is relevant to our proposal in this paper. As mentioned in section 1, a proposition (which corresponds to a semantic representation of a sentence) is regarded as a *type* in DTS. In our analysis, we use the following four type constructors (in the DTS notation) which are also used in the previous study on formal semantics based on dependent type theory (Ranta, 1994; Luo, 2012; Bekki and Mineshima, 2017).

- Π-type: $(x\colon A) \to B(x)$
- Σ-type: $(x : A) \times B$, also written as $\begin{bmatrix} x : A \\ B(x) \end{bmatrix}$
- Disjoint Union Type ($\uplus$-type): $A \uplus B$

$$\dfrac{\dfrac{\overline{x:A}^{\,k}}{\vdots} \quad A : type_i \quad B : type_j}{(x\colon A) \bigoplus B : type_{max(i,j)}} (\bigoplus F), k \qquad \dfrac{t : A \quad u : B[t/x]}{[t,u] : (x\colon A) \bigoplus B} (\bigoplus I) \qquad \dfrac{[t,u] : (x\colon A) \bigoplus B \quad \dfrac{\overline{x:A}^{\,k} \; \overline{y:B(x)}^{\,k}}{\vdots} \; m : C}{case_{[t,u]} m : C} (\bigoplus E), k$$

Figure 2: Inference rules of existential type. Elimination rule $(\bigoplus E)$ can be applied if $m : C$ and any open assumption on which $m : C$ depends do not contain x and y as free variables.

- Enumeration Type ({ }-type): $\{a_1, a_2, \ldots, a_n\}$

Figure 1 shows inference rules for these types. Π-type and Σ-type can be considered as generalized function type and generalized product type, respectively. These two types make a difference from simple type theory where only non-dependent function type $A \to B$ and product type $A \times B$ are admitted. $\uplus$-type is a disjoint union type. We also use enumeration type ({ }-type), written $\{a_1, a_2, \ldots, a_n\}$, to express the finite domain of entities; this setting is essential for our implementation, which we will discuss in section 5. The bottom type $\bot$ is defined as { }, i.e., the enumeration type inhabited by no term. The bottom type $\bot$ is used for defining the negation of A; as usual, $\neg A$ is defined as $A \to \bot$.

In addition, we use *existential type* (also called weak-sigma type) (Luo, 1994), written $(x\colon A) \bigoplus B$, for semantic representations of wh-questions. Figure 2 shows inference rules of $\bigoplus$-type. Existential type corresponds to existential quantification in intuitionistic logic. The difference between Σ-type and $\bigoplus$-type is in elimination rule. The elimination rule of Σ-type allows to use projections (see ΣE in Figure 1), while the elimination rule of $\bigoplus$-type (see $\bigoplus E$ in Figure 2) does not. Thus, a pair of terms $[t, u]$ which is a proof term of $(x\colon A) \bigoplus B$ cannot be divided into t and u by applying projection.

One of the other features of DTS is that expressions that trigger presupposition and anaphora are uniformly treated as underspecified terms, written @ (See Bekki and Mineshima (2017) for the detail). In our extension of DTS with interrogative semantics, this uniform treatment of anaphora and presupposition in terms of underspecification is preserved.

3 Semantic Representations for Interrogatives

In this section, we introduce semantic representations of interrogative sentences. We focus on three types of questions: polar question, alternative question and wh-question. Before we explain the detail of semantics of interrogative sentences in DTS, we show how to characterize the relationships between questions and their answers in our framework.

Partly building on Inquisitive Semantics (Ciardelli et al., 2019), we treat questions and assertions as having the same type in our type-theoretic framework. Also following Inquisitive Semantics, we define the entailment relation holding between a semantic representation (SR) of a declarative sentence and that of an interrogative sentence: the SR S_1 of a declarative sentence is an answer to the SR S_2 of an interrogative sentence if and only if S_1 entails S_2 in DTS. Using this definition, we can describe question-answer relationship as entailment relation and evaluate our semantic representations by a testset for question-answering.

3.1 Basic Declarative Sentence

We start with semantic representations of basic declarative sentences in DTS. Σ-type represents existential sentences; for instance, (1b) is a semantic representation of (1a). Σ-type is used to capture *externally dynamic* character of existential quantification in the sense of Groenendijk and Stokhof (1991); we will come back to this point later.

(1) a. Someone ran.

b. $\begin{bmatrix} x : \text{Entity} \\ \textbf{run}(x) \end{bmatrix}$

Another type of basic declarative sentence we need to introduce is a universal sentence like (2a). The semantic representation of (2a) is given in (2b). Universal propositions are analyzed using Π-type.

(2) a. Every student ran.

b. $\left(u : \begin{bmatrix} x : \text{Entity} \\ \textbf{student}(x) \end{bmatrix}\right) \to \textbf{run}(\pi_1(u))$

3.2 Wh-Question

There are two different interpretations of wh-question, called *mention-some* reading and *mention-all* reading (Dayal, 2016). For instance, (3a) and (3b) are examples of wh-questions having a mention-some reading and a mention-all reading, respectively.

(3) a. What is something that Alice really likes?

b. Who did Alice invite to her birthday party?

An answer to a mention-some wh-question is characterized by an instance satisfying the property in question; thus it does not have to mention all instances which satisfy the property. For example, if Alice likes chocolate, football and mathematics, (4a) and (4b) can be regarded as an answer to the mention-some wh-question in (3a), that is, an answer to (3a) is characterized by mentioning some entity which Alice likes.

(4) a. Alice likes chocolate.

b. Alice likes football.

An answer to a mention-all question has to be exhaustive, that is, it must provide complete information about the question in the relevant domain. Thus, if Alice invited only Susan and John to her birthday party, (5a) is an answer to (3b). By contrast, (5b) and (5c) are not suited for an answer to (3b) because they do not give an exhaustive answer.

(5) a. Alice invited only Susan and John to her birthday party.

b. Alice invited Susan.

c. Alice invited John.

For representing the meaning of a mention-some wh-question, we use existential type ($\bigoplus$-type). For the sake of illustration, consider a simple mention-some wh-question in (6a), whose semantic representation is given in (6b).

(6) a. Who ran? (mention-some reading)

b. $(x\colon \text{Entity}) \bigoplus \textbf{run}(x)$

The existential sentence in (1a) can be a (at least semantically) proper answer to the mention-some wh-question. Thus the entailment relation in (7a) should hold. What is crucial here is that declarative existential sentences are analyzed as Σ-types, while mention-some wh-questions are analyzed as existential types. Thus, our analysis correctly derives the relation as stated in (7b); the SR of (1a) entails the SR of (6a), but not vice versa.[4]

(7) a. Someone ran. ⇒ Who ran? (mention-some)

b. $\begin{bmatrix} x : \text{Entity} \\ \textbf{run}(x) \end{bmatrix} \vdash (x\colon \text{Entity}) \bigoplus \textbf{run}(x)$

As shown in Figure 1 and Figure 2, Σ-type and $\bigoplus$-type have the same formation and introduction rules. As is mentioned in Section 2, the difference is in elimination rule. This causes differences in anaphora resolution between (8a) and (8b).

[4]It is widely accepted that mention-some wh-question has an existential presupposition (Dayal, 2016). Here we assume that a mention-some wh-question does not entail the corresponding existential sentence but just presupposes it.

(8) a. Someone$_i$ ran. He$_i$ is a student.

b. Who$_i$ ran? (mention-some) # He$_i$ is a student.

An existential proposition introduces an entity which can be referred to in the subsequent sentences (Groenendijk and Stokhof, 1991). This externally dynamic character of existential quantification is captured by means of Σ-types (Ranta, 1994; Bekki and Mineshima, 2017; Tanaka et al., 2018). Thus, the mini-discourse in (8a) can be given the following full interpretation in DTS.[5]

(9) $$\begin{bmatrix} u : \begin{bmatrix} x : \text{Entity} \\ \textbf{run}(x) \end{bmatrix} \\ \textbf{student}(\pi_1(u)) \end{bmatrix}$$

Here, u introduced by the Σ-type is a pair of an entity x and a proof that x is a student. Thus the projection $\pi_1(u)$, which is allowed by the elimination rule of Σ-type (see Figure 1), successfully picks up its first component (the entity x), which can be used in the subsequent discourse.

In contrast, the elimination rule of $\bigoplus$-type (see Figure 2) does not provide a projection function. Thus this makes it impossible to establish the anaphoric link for (8b), which is a desirable prediction. There is no way to pass an entity introduced by the SR in (10) to the subsequent sentences.

(10) $(x\colon \text{Entity}) \bigoplus \textbf{run}(x)$

Let us move on to the semantic representations of mention-all wh-question in our framework. For instance, consider the question in (11a). The mention-all reading of this question can be represented using Π-type and disjoint union type as in (11b).

(11) a. Who ran? (mention-all)

b. $(x\colon \text{Entity}) \to (\textbf{run}(x) \uplus \neg\textbf{run}(x))$

As is in other systems based on dependent types, our underlying proof system is based on intuitionistic logic where the law of excluded middle is not allowed. Therefore, (11b) is not a theorem. A proof for the SR in (11b) is a function f such that for any entity x, $f(x)$ is a proof of $\textbf{run}(x)$ or a proof of $\neg\textbf{run}(x)$. That is to say, to prove the SR in (11b), one has to know whether x runs or not for each entity x in the domain. This naturally captures the answering condition for the mention-all reading of (11a). Note that (12b) can serve as an answer to this mention-all question.

(12) a. Only John ran.

b. $((x\colon \text{Entity}) \to (\textbf{run}(x) \to (x = \textbf{j}))) \wedge \textbf{run}(\textbf{j})$

The SR in (12b) means that John ran and the other entities did not run. We may assume that the number of entities in the domain is finite, which can be expressed by using enumeration type ($\{\}$-type). In this setting, (12b) entails (11b) in DTS; thus this correctly predicts that (12a) is an answer to (11a).

3.3 Polar Question

Semantic representations of polar question are given by using $\uplus$-type. (13a) is a simple example of polar question and (13b) is its semantic representation.

(13) a. Did John run?

b. $\textbf{run}(\textbf{j}) \uplus \neg\textbf{run}(\textbf{j})$

In the same manner as in (11), our analysis derives the entailment in (14b), thus correctly predicting that *John ran* is an answer to the polar question in (13a).

(14) a. John ran. $\Rightarrow$ Did John run?

b. $\textbf{run}(\textbf{j}) \vdash \textbf{run}(\textbf{j}) \uplus \neg\textbf{run}(\textbf{j})$

[5] For the detail on how to derive this interpretation using underspecified terms in DTS, see Tanaka et al. (2018).

3.4 Alternative Question

The semantic representations of alternative questions are also given by using $\uplus$-type. While the semantic representation of a polar question automatically meets the exhaustiveness condition by using $\uplus$-type, some alternative questions need to express exhaustiveness explicitly. Here we assume that *neither* and *both* are not a suitable answer to an alternative question like (15a).[6] We use (15b) as the semantic representation of (15a).

(15) a. Did John run or walk ?

b. $\mathbf{run(j)} \uplus \mathbf{walk(j)}$
$\wedge\ (\mathbf{run(j)} \rightarrow (\neg \mathbf{walk(j)}))$
$\wedge\ (\mathbf{walk(j)} \rightarrow (\neg \mathbf{run(j)}))$

Under this analysis, it can be shown that (16a), whose semantic representation is given in (16b), is an answer to (15a).

(16) a. John ran and didn't walk.

b. $\mathbf{run(j)} \wedge \neg \mathbf{walk(j)}$

In Inquisitive Semantics, alternative questions and declarative sentences with *or* are logically distinguished by means of double negation (Ciardelli et al., 2019). This option is not available in our framework, because double negation wrongly blocks a certain type of potential anaphoric links in DTS. As an example, consider the mini-discourse in (17a). The semantic representation of the first sentence of (17a) is given in (17b).

(17) a. Susan$_i$ saw a horse$_j$ or a pony$_j$. She$_i$waved to it$_j$.

b.
$$\begin{bmatrix} u : \begin{bmatrix} x : \text{Entity} \\ \mathbf{horse}(x) \end{bmatrix} \\ \mathbf{see}(\mathbf{s}, \pi_1 u) \end{bmatrix} \uplus \begin{bmatrix} u : \begin{bmatrix} x : \text{Entity} \\ \mathbf{pony}(x) \end{bmatrix} \\ \mathbf{see}(\mathbf{s}, \pi_1 u) \end{bmatrix}$$
$$\wedge \left(\begin{bmatrix} u : \begin{bmatrix} x : \text{Entity} \\ \mathbf{horse}(x) \end{bmatrix} \\ \mathbf{see}(\mathbf{s}, \pi_1 u) \end{bmatrix} \rightarrow \neg \begin{bmatrix} u : \begin{bmatrix} x : \text{Entity} \\ \mathbf{pony}(x) \end{bmatrix} \\ \mathbf{see}(\mathbf{s}, \pi_1 u) \end{bmatrix} \right)$$
$$\wedge \left(\begin{bmatrix} u : \begin{bmatrix} x : \text{Entity} \\ \mathbf{pony}(x) \end{bmatrix} \\ \mathbf{see}(\mathbf{s}, \pi_1 u) \end{bmatrix} \rightarrow \neg \begin{bmatrix} u : \begin{bmatrix} x : \text{Entity} \\ \mathbf{horse}(x) \end{bmatrix} \\ \mathbf{see}(\mathbf{s}, \pi_1 u) \end{bmatrix} \right)$$

If the semantic representation of the first sentence of (17a) is the one obtained by applying double negation to (17b), then it predicts that the anaphoric link in (17a) is impossible, contrary to the fact. For this reason, we do not use double negation for distinguishing alternative question from declarative disjunctive sentence.

4 Compositional Semantics

In this section, we provide a brief overview of how to compose semantic representations of sentences in DTS. For concreteness, we use CCG as a syntactic component of our framework. Table 1 shows an excerpt from the lexical entries we implement in this study.[7] For convenience, we assume that the category NP is always type-raised; the type-raised categories $(S/(S\backslash NP))$ and $(S\backslash(S/NP))$ are abbreviated as $NP^{\uparrow}_{nom}$ and $NP^{\uparrow}_{acc}$, respectively. (18) is a simple example of the derivation tree annotated with semantic representations.

[6]See Biezma and Rawlins (2012) for discussion on the status of "neither" and "both" as an answer to alternative questions.

[7]All the codes to implement our system and the testset used in the experiments are available at `https://github.com/Kazuuuuuki/DTS-question-parser`.

PF	Category	Semantic representation
John	$NP^{\uparrow}_{nom\|acc}$	$\lambda p.p(\mathbf{j})$
	$S_{or}/(S_{or}\backslash NP)$	$\lambda p.p(\mathbf{j})$
everyone	$NP^{\uparrow}_{nom\|acc}$	$\lambda p.\,(x\colon \text{Entity}) \to p(x)$
someone	$NP^{\uparrow}_{nom\|acc}$	$\lambda p.\begin{bmatrix} x : \text{Entity} \\ p(x) \end{bmatrix}$
nobody	$NP^{\uparrow}_{nom\|acc}$	$\lambda p.\,(x\colon \text{Entity}) \to \neg p(x)$
every	$NP^{\uparrow}_{nom\|acc}/N$	$\lambda n.\lambda p.\left(v\colon \begin{bmatrix} y : \text{Entity} \\ ny \end{bmatrix}\right) \to p(\pi_1(v))$
a, some	$NP^{\uparrow}_{nom\|acc}/N$	$\lambda n.\lambda p.\begin{bmatrix} v : \begin{bmatrix} y : \text{Entity} \\ ny \end{bmatrix} \\ p(\pi_1(v)) \end{bmatrix}$
only	$NP^{\uparrow}_{nom}/NP^{\uparrow}_{nom}$	$\lambda P.\lambda q.((x\colon \text{Entity}) \to (q(x) \to P(\lambda y.y) = x)) \wedge P(q)$
	$NP^{\uparrow}_{acc}/NP^{\uparrow}_{acc}$	$\lambda P.\lambda q.((x\colon \text{Entity}) \to (q(x) \to P(\lambda y.y) = x)) \wedge P(q)$
student	N	**student**
walk	$S\backslash NP$	**walk**
run	$S\backslash NP$	**run**
see	$S\backslash NP^{\uparrow}_{nom}/NP^{\uparrow}_{acc}$	$\lambda Q.\lambda P.P(\lambda x.Q(\lambda y.\mathbf{see}(x,y)))$
or	$(S\backslash S)/S$	$\lambda S1.\lambda S2.S1 \uplus S2$
	$(S_{or}\backslash S)/S$	$\lambda S1.\lambda S2.((S1 \uplus S2) \wedge (S1 \to \neg S2) \wedge (S2 \to \neg S1))$
	$((S\backslash NP)\backslash(S\backslash NP))/(S\backslash NP)$	$\lambda p.\lambda q.\lambda x.(q(x) \uplus p(x))$
	$((S_{or}\backslash NP)\backslash(S\backslash NP))/(S\backslash NP)$	$\lambda p.\lambda q.\lambda x.(q(x) \uplus p(x)) \wedge (q(x) \to \neg p(x)) \wedge (p(x) \to \neg q(x))$
and	$(S\backslash S)/S$	$\lambda S1.\lambda S2.S1 \wedge S2$
	$(NP^{\uparrow}_{nom}\backslash NP^{\uparrow}_{nom})/NP^{\uparrow}_{nom}$	$\lambda P.\lambda Q.\lambda r.P(r) \wedge Q(r)$
	$(NP^{\uparrow}_{acc}\backslash NP^{\uparrow}_{acc})/NP^{\uparrow}_{acc}$	$\lambda P.\lambda Q.\lambda r.P(r) \wedge Q(r)$
who	$S_{some}/(S\backslash NP)$	$\lambda p.\,(x\colon \text{Entity}) \bigoplus p(x)$
	$S_{all}/(S\backslash NP)$	$\lambda p.\,(x\colon \text{Entity}) \to p(x) \uplus \neg p(x)$
	$S_{some}/((S\backslash NP^{\uparrow}_{nom}/NP^{\uparrow}_{acc})/NP^{\uparrow}_{nom}$	$\lambda P.\lambda Q.Q(\lambda Q1.\begin{bmatrix} x : \text{Entity} \\ Q1(x) \end{bmatrix}(P))$
do	S/S	$\lambda S.S$
	S_{or}/S_{or}	$\lambda S.S$
did	S/S	$\lambda S.S$
	S_{or}/S_{or}	$\lambda S.S$
?	$S\backslash S$	$\lambda S.(S \uplus \neg S)$
	$S\backslash S_{some}$	$\lambda S.S$
	$S\backslash S_{or}$	$\lambda S.S$
	$S\backslash S_{all}$	$\lambda S.S$

Table 1: An excerpt from the lexical entries for our interrogative semantics.

(18) John saw Susan.

$$\dfrac{\dfrac{\text{John}}{\begin{array}{c} NP^{\uparrow}_{nom} \\ \lambda p.p(\mathbf{j}) \end{array}} \qquad \dfrac{\dfrac{\text{saw}}{\begin{array}{c} (S\backslash NP^{\uparrow}_{nom})/NP^{\uparrow}_{acc} \\ \lambda Q.\lambda P.P(\lambda x.Q(\lambda y.\mathbf{see}(x,y))) \end{array}} \qquad \dfrac{\text{Susan}}{\begin{array}{c} NP^{\uparrow}_{acc} \\ \lambda p.p(\mathbf{s}) \end{array}}}{\begin{array}{c} S\backslash NP^{\uparrow}_{nom} \\ \lambda P.P(\lambda x.\mathbf{see}(x,\mathbf{s})) \end{array}}>}{\begin{array}{c} S \\ \mathbf{see}(\mathbf{j},\mathbf{s}) \end{array}}<$$

As an example of a simple polar question, consider (19). The CCG derivation of (19) shows that the question mark "?" induces inquisitive meaning for polar questions.

(19) Did John run?

$$\dfrac{\dfrac{\dfrac{\text{Did}}{\begin{array}{c} S/S \\ \lambda S.S \end{array}} \qquad \dfrac{\dfrac{\text{John}}{\begin{array}{c} NP^{\uparrow}_{nom} \\ \lambda p.p(\mathbf{j}) \end{array}} \qquad \dfrac{\text{run}}{\begin{array}{c} S\backslash NP \\ \lambda x.\mathbf{run}(x) \end{array}}}{\begin{array}{c} S \\ \mathbf{run}(\mathbf{j}) \end{array}}>}{\begin{array}{c} S \\ \mathbf{run}(\mathbf{j}) \end{array}}> \qquad \dfrac{?}{\begin{array}{c} S\backslash S \\ \lambda S.(S \uplus \neg S) \end{array}}}{\begin{array}{c} S \\ (\mathbf{run}(\mathbf{j}) \uplus \neg \mathbf{run}(\mathbf{j})) \end{array}}<$$

As a more involved case, (20) is a derivation tree for a declarative sentence with *or* and (21) for an alternative question with *or*. Note that we use different categories for *or* in (20) and (21).

(20) John ran or walked.

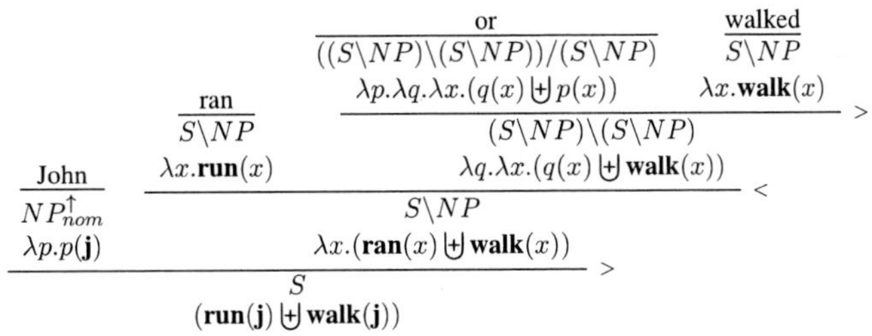

(21) Did John run or walk ?

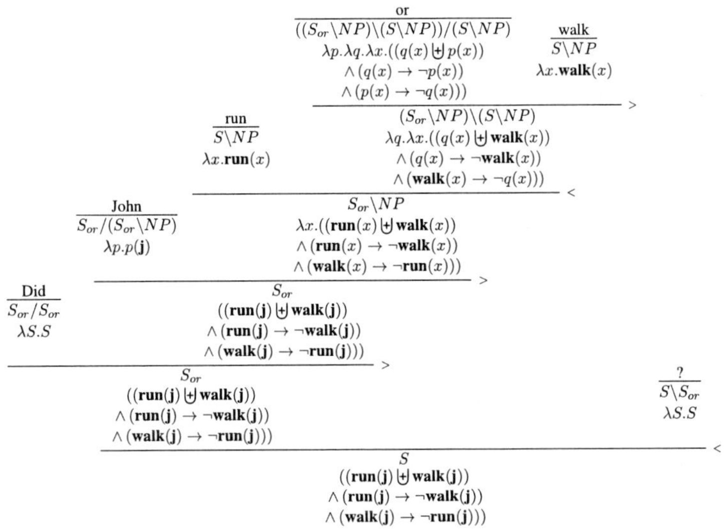

In (21), *or* introduces a category with a feature S_{or}, which is taken over to the node of category S_{or} for *Did John run or walk*; then the question mark "?" of category $S\backslash S_{or}$ takes it as argument and returns an expression of category S. Thus the question mark "?" does not introduce inquisitive meaning if it takes an expression of category S_{or}.

The reason for assigning several different categories to a question mark can be seen by considering (22).[8] The semantic representation of (22) is one for an alternative question in the same way as (21). Thus the inquisitive meaning is introduced not by the question mark "?" but by *or* of alternative question.

(22) Did John run or did he walk ?

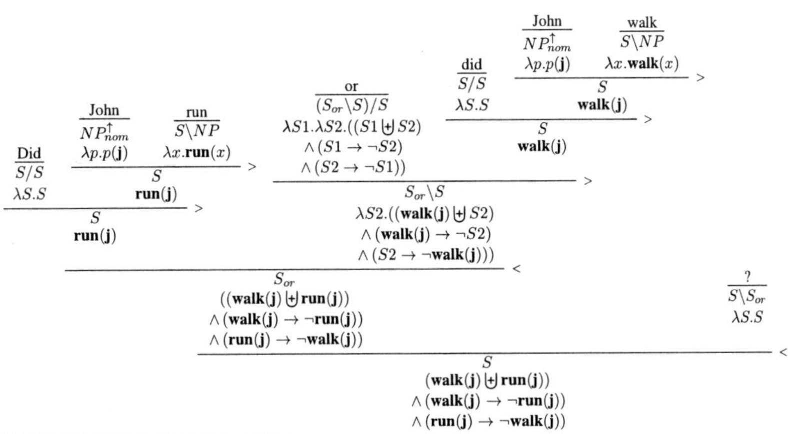

[8] In the derivation tree of (22), *he* is converted to *John* for simplicity.

Answer (Premise)	Question (Conclusion)	Label
John ran.	Who ran ? (mention-some)	yes
Someone ran.	Who ran ? (mention-some)	yes
Only John saw Susan.	Who saw Susan ? (mention-all)	yes
John ran or Susan walked.	Who ran ? (mention-some)	unknown
Nobody ran.	Who ran ? (mention-some)	no
Nobody ran.	Who ran ? (mention-all)	yes
Only John ran.	Who didn't run ? (mention-all)	yes
John didn't run.	Who ran ? (mention-some)	unknown
Every student ran.	Did John run ?	yes
John ran or Susan walked.	Did John run ?	unknown
John ran and Susan walked.	Did John run ?	yes
John didn't run.	Did John run ?	yes
Only John ran.	Did John run ?	yes
John ran or walked.	Did John run or walk?	unknown
John ran and didn't walk.	Did John run or did John walk ?	yes
Nobody ran.	Did John run?	yes
John is tall and John is not short.	Is John tall or short ?	yes

Table 2: Some examples from our testset. We assume that the denotation of *student* consists of John and Susan.

5 Experiment

We implement the compositional semantics introduced in the previous section using ccg2lambda. Since there is a non-trivial gap between the outputs of the state-of-the-art CCG parsers (e.g., Yoshikawa et al., 2017) and the syntactic structures we assume in this study, we manually annotate CCG trees for the input sentences. We implement the compositional mapping from CCG trees to the semantic representations discussed so far, using the lexical entries presented in the previous section.[9] The system automatically converts an input CCG tree to the corresponding semantic representation in DTS.

Implementation of a proof system is also needed for checking the relationships between answers and questions formulated as entailment relation. We use Ltac (Delahaye, 2000), a tactic language available in Coq to implement proof automation necessary for our purposes.

We built a testset consisting of 49 question-answer pairs. Some examples are shown in Table 2. Each problem in the testset has two sentences; the first sentence is an answer and the second sentence is a question. For each pair of the testset, we annotated a gold CCG tree. Here is an example for an answer sentence *Everyone runs* and a question sentence *Who ran ?* (mention-some reading):

(23)
```
(S (<S/<S\NP>> Everyone) (S\NP run))
(S (S_some (<S_some/<S\NP>> Who_some) (S\NP run)) (S\S_some ?))
```

The answer to each problem is *yes* (entailment), *no* (contradiction), or *unknown* (neither), following the FraCaS testset (Cooper et al., 1994). The distribution of answers is: yes/no/unknown = 36/1/12 For evaluating the basic capacity of compositional semantics and proof system, we keep the sentences included in the testset as simple as possible. This makes easy to detect what phenomena a given system fails to give an appropriate semantic representation.

In the setting for theorem proving in Coq, we use a finite domain with three entities: John, Susan and Lucy. This can be implemented using enumeration type in Coq:

(24)
```
Inductive Entity : Type := | John | Susan | Lucy.
```

[9] The distinction between *mention-some* and *mentione-all* readings is annotated to wh-expressions; see entries for *who* in Table 1.

The Coq script automatically generated for the CCG trees for the question-answer pair in (23) is the following:

(25) `(forall x:Entity,(_run x)) -> (ex Entity (fun x => (_run x)))`

Here the semantic representation for the answer sentence appears in the antecedent of implication "->" and that for the question sentence appears in the consequent. We use existential type in Coq, written `ex`, for representing mention-some wh-question. The system correctly proves (25) as a theorem.

In this setting, we can successfully derive the desired semantic representations and prove the entailment relations for all 49 cases.

6 Conclusion

In this paper, we extended the framework of DTS with semantics for a variety of interrogative sentences. There are many topics which cannot be discussed in this paper. Among others, we do not deal with embedded questions. Also, we do not give a detailed examination of the presuppositions of wh-questions in the context of DTS. Tanaka et al. (2017) presented an analysis of factive verbs like *know* in the framekwork of DTS, but the relationship between our proposal and this work is not obvious yet. These issues will be left for future work.

Acknowledgement

This work was partially supported by JSPS KAKENHI Grant Number JP18H03284 Japan, and JST CREST Grant Number JPMJCR1301 Japan. We thank the three anonymous reviewers for their helpful comments.

References

Bekki, D. (2014). Representing anaphora with dependent types. In *Logical Aspects of Computational Linguistics (8th international conference)*, pp. 14–29. Springer.

Bekki, D. and K. Mineshima (2017). Context-passing and underspecification in Dependent Type Semantics. In *Modern Perspectives in Type Theoretical Semantics, Studies in Linguistics and Philosophy*, pp. 11–41. Springer.

Biezma, M. and K. Rawlins (2012). Responding to alternative and polar questions. *Linguistics and Philosophy 35*(5), 361–406.

Chatzikyriakidis, S. and Z. Luo (2014). Natural language inference in Coq. *Journal of Logic, Language and Information 23*(4), 441–480.

Chatzikyriakidis, S. and Z. Luo (2017). *Modern Perspectives in Type-Theoretical Semantics*. Springer.

Ciardelli, I., J. Groenendijk, and F. Roelofsen (2019). *Inquisitive semantics*. Oxford University Press.

Cooper, R. (2012). Type theory and semantics in flux. *Handbook of the Philosophy of Science 14*, 271–323.

Cooper, R., R. Crouch, J. Van Eijck, C. Fox, J. Van Genabith, J. Jaspers, H. Kamp, M. Pinkal, M. Poesio, S. Pulman, et al. (1994). FraCaS: A framework for computational semantics. *Deliverable D6.*

Dayal, V. (2016). *Questions*. Oxford University Press.

Delahaye, D. (2000). A tactic language for the system coq. In *International Conference on Logic for Programming Artificial Intelligence and Reasoning*, pp. 85–95. Springer.

Ginzburg, J. (2005). Abstraction and ontology: Questions as propositional abstracts in type theory with records. *Journal of Logic and Computation 15*, 113–130.

Groenendijk, J. and M. Stokhof (1991). Dynamic predicate logic. *Linguistics and philosophy 14*(1), 39–100.

Luo, Z. (1994). *Computation and Reasoning: A Type Theory for Computer Science.* Oxford University Press.

Luo, Z. (2012). Formal semantics in modern type theories with coercive subtyping. *Linguistics and Philosophy 35*(6), 491–513.

Martin-Löf, P. (1984). *Intuitionistic Type Theory.* Bibliopolis.

Martínez-Gómez, P., K. Mineshima, Y. Miyao, and D. Bekki (2016). ccg2lambda: A compositional semantics system. In *Proceedings of ACL 2016 System Demonstrations*, pp. 85–90. Association for Computational Linguistics.

Ranta, A. (1994). *Type-Theoretical Grammar.* Oxford University Press.

Steedman, M. (1996). *Surface Structure and Interpretation.* MIT Press.

Tanaka, R., K. Mineshima, and D. Bekki (2017). Factivity and presupposition in dependent type semantics. *Journal of Language Modelling 5*(2), 385–420.

Tanaka, R., K. Mineshima, and D. Bekki (2018). Paychecks, presupposition, and dependent types. In *Fifth Workshop on Natural Language and Computer Science (NLCS 2018).*

The Coq Development Team (2016). The Coq Proof Assistant: Reference Manual: Version 8.5.pl3.

Yoshikawa, M., H. Noji, and Y. Matsumoto (2017). A* CCG parsing with a supertag and dependency factored model. In *Proceedings of the 55th Annual Meeting of the Association for Computational Linguistics (Volume 1: Long Papers)*, pp. 277–287. Association for Computational Linguistics.

Monads for hyperintensionality? A situation semantics for hyperintensional side effects and intra-sentential anaphora

Luke Burke – *University of Bamberg* and *University College London*

20th April, 2019

P-HYPE, the semantic theory we outline, uses monads from category theory in order to integrate a perspective-sensitive semantic theory with a hyperintensional logic, HYPE (Leitgeb 2018). This enables us to to capture in a fine-grained way the utterer's perspective on other people's perspectives, a phenomenon that (Asudeh and Giorgolo 2016) argue plays a role in natural language. But it also enables us to construct a particular approach to hyperintensionality in natural language within HYPE, since HYPE itself is compatible with different accounts of hyperintensionality in natural language. In P-HYPE, hyperintensionality is modelled as a side effect in the sense of (Charlow 2014) and of consisting in a special type of perspective sensitivity. P-HYPE builds on the account of (Asudeh and Giorgolo 2016), by carving out a notion of perspectives as special sets of situations which can be combined together via a fusion relation. In addition, we briefly illustrate how we can combine P-HYPE with an account of certain kinds of intra-sentential anaphora.

Keywords: Attitude verbs, monads, side effects, perspective, hyperintensionality, situation semantics

1. Introduction: Hyperintensionality as a side effect

So-called 'hyperintensional' semantic theories allow us to block the free substitution of intensionally equivalent sentences (see (Fox and Lappin 2008) and references therein), such as tautologies and mathematical truths, which, at least in standard frameworks used in natural language semantics (Gallin 1975), express the same function from worlds to truth values. The phenomenon of hyperintensionality might therefore be thought to constitute a 'compositionality challenge' (Zimmermann 2012), in that the naïf semantics employed in standard frameworks cannot compositionally account for the different meaning of distinct mathematical/logical truths and we lack an agreed-upon method of compositionally deriving their meanings. (Shan 2002) had the intuition that we can model many seemingly non-compositional phenomena by using monads, as 'side effects' of computing the main value of an expression. Subsequently, certain linguistic phenomena exhibiting non-determinism, intensionality or state-changing operators have been captured via monads (Charlow 2014). We propose that hyperintensionality be added to this list as a particular kind of side effect, in the sense of (Charlow 2014) and (Shan 2007). (Shan 2007) in particular, includes amongst so-called *linguistic side effects* certain types of referential opacity and certain expressions whose meaning and compositional contribution is not pre-theoretically transparent. Hyperintensionality is arguably a good example of a linguistic side effect in Shan's sense, since it is not clear what distinction to make between the semantic contribution of logically equivalent statements, how their meanings relate to their truth conditions, and how to characterise their behaviour compositionally. But from both (Charlow 2014) and Shan's list of linguistic side effects, hyperintensionality is conspicuous by its absence. It is high time to fit hyperintensionality into the monadic fold.

Cue the entry of HYPE (Leitgeb 2018), which we discuss in detail later. HYPE is hyperintensional, but does not offer on its own a completely satisfying analysis of hyperintensionality in natural language (as

(Leitgeb 2018) points out regarding verbs like *believe*, which he calls 'quasi-syntactic'[1]).[2] For example, $A \to (B \to A)$ is an axiom in HYPE, and so true in all states of every HYPE model. Likewise, $A \to A$ is an axiom of HYPE. But someone might not believe $A \to (B \to A)$, for certain A, B. And, again instantiating sentences for A and B, $A \to (B \to A)$ and $A \to A$ might differ in meaning, even though they are logically equivalent in HYPE.[3] No doubt these problems could be circumvented by a theory of natural language hyperintensionality in HYPE.[4] That is precisely what we are providing here (however in (Burke 2019) we discuss the particular problem just mentioned), but incorporating perspective sensitivity into HYPE itself. Both P-HYPE and the semantics of (Asudeh and Giorgolo 2016) (from now on *AG*), enrich the typed lambda calculus with a reader monad (Shan 2002) defined on the type p, of perspective indices. We will discuss how perspective indices are employed later. For now we can just say that to every agent in a discourse there corresponds a perspective index, and that certain terms which are perspective sensitive are interpreted relative to perspective indices. If an expression has type α, a perspectivally sensitive expression has type $p \to \alpha$. The reader monad is a triple $(\Diamond, \eta, \bigstar)$. $\Diamond : TYPE \to TYPE$, is a type-constructor, which behaves as a special modal operator in Lax logic (Fairtlough and Mendler 1997).[5] $\Diamond$ maps any type τ to $p \to \tau$ and, for all a, b, maps a function $f : a \to b$ to a function $\Diamond f : \Diamond a \to \Diamond b$, such that $(\Diamond f)(x) = \lambda i.f(xi)$.[6] $\eta : \tau \to \Diamond\tau$ is a value-constructor that takes a non-monadic value $x : \tau$ and trivially upgrades it to monadic values by forming a constant function from perspective indices to x. It is called the *unit* of the monad:

Definition 1 : $\eta(x) =_{def} \lambda i.x : p \to \alpha$ (1) $\bigstar$ ('bind'): $\Diamond\tau \to (\tau \to \Diamond\delta) \to \Diamond\delta$

Finally, $\bigstar$ (called *bind*) is a polymorphic binary infix operator acting as a sort of functional application:

Definition 2 : $a\bigstar f =_{def} \lambda i.f(a(i))(i)$ where $a : \Diamond\tau, f : \tau \to \Diamond\delta$

1.1. AG's semantic theory

Consider the sentence (2a), uttered in the scenario (2b)

(2) a. Mary Jane loves Spiderman.
   b. *Scenario:* Mary Jane does not know Peter Parker's secret identity and loves the man she calls 'Peter Parker'. A speaker σ who knows or is 'enlightened' (Zimmermann 2005) about Peter Parker's secret identity utters (2a)

According to AG, there is a sense in which (2a) is true, from the perspective of an enlightened utterer, but false from Mary Jane's perspective. (Asudeh and Giorgolo 2016) model this by making certain names perspective relative, so that Mary Jane can associate a distinct denotation with the names 'Spiderman' and 'Peter Parker'. Thus names denote certain people's mental representations-*perspectives*. We can then imagine a private mental lexicon for each person, consisting of the set of perspectives that a given person associates with terms of her language, which we call that person's perspective. We use 'perspective' ambiguously–both to denote a semantic value in someone's lexicon, and that person's lexicon itself–with the context serving to disambiguate which notion we have

[1] "Once again, the logic and semantics of the system HYPE to be developed in the present article would not be able to contribute to investigations into hyperintensional operators of any such quasi-syntactic kind."(Leitgeb 2018)

[2] A reviewer asks why HYPE is not sufficient to account for hyperintensionality. This paragraph gives some reasons for this conclusion. Another reviewer also writes that HYPE is already hyperintensional, so adding another device (perspectives) for hyperintensionality should be carefully argued for. This paragraph should also be relevant to her question.

[3] For example, 'If I will be late then if I have a coffee then I will be late' has a different meaning from 'If I am late then I am late'. Other examples could be given not involving conditional connectives.

[4] In (Burke 2019) we show that such examples can be dealt with both with HYPE and with P-HYPE. But P-HYPE in addition accounts for a variety of data involving perspective relativity, so is *ceterus paribus* preferable.

[5] It is an endofunctor, as this is understood in Category theory; that is, a functor that maps a category to itself (in this case the category of types).

[6] Throughout '$x : \alpha$' is read 'x is of type α'

WORD	DENOTATION	TYPE
Mary Jane	$\mathbf{mj}_\sigma$	e
Peter Parker	$\mathbf{pp}_\sigma$	e
believe	$\lambda c.\lambda s.\mathbf{B}(s, c(\kappa(s)))$	$\Diamond t \to e \to t$
love	$\lambda o.\lambda s.\mathbf{love}(s, o(\kappa(s)))$	$\Diamond e \to e \to t$
Spider-Man	$\lambda i. \begin{cases} \mathbf{sm(i)} & \text{if } i = \kappa(mj) \\ \mathbf{pp(i)} & \text{if } i = \kappa(\sigma) \end{cases}$	$\Diamond e$

Table 1 Lexicon of σ, the enlightened speaker

in mind. Consider the lexicon (**Table 1**) of the enlightened speaker σ of (2a). Plain names are subscripted with σ to indicate that this is the denotation of that name for σ. The names which are type $\Diamond e$ have different denotations, depending on the perspective index they are fed. AG suppose that certain names vary in perspective but others do not. Those which do not vary in perspective have something like a default status, in the following sense: if someone becomes enlightened, and learns, for example that Spiderman and Peter Parker are one and the same thing, then they will, by and large, just use plain 'Peter Parker', and this name will thence have default status, with 'Spiderman'.[7] Notice the κ operator in the denotation of *believe* and *love*. κ has the following interpretation (where D_e is the domain of individuals of a model):

(3) $\forall x \in D_e\ (\kappa(x) \in P)$

Perspective sensitive expressions that scope below κ are interpreted relative to the perspective index corresponding to the subject of the attitude report (see **Table 1**). Expressions that scope above $\bigstar$, are interpreted relative to the default perspective of the utterer. Let us consider the two readings of (2a). The false reading of (2a) is represented by (4),which β-reduces to (5), and the true reading is represented by (6), which β-reduces to (7):

(4) $$love(mj_\sigma, \lambda i. \begin{cases} \mathbf{sm(i)} & \text{if } i = \kappa(mj) \\ \mathbf{pp(i)} & \text{if } i = \kappa(\sigma) \end{cases} (\kappa(mj)))$$

(5) $$love(mj_\sigma, sm(\kappa(mj)))$$

(6) $$\left(\lambda i. \begin{cases} \mathbf{sm(i)} & \text{if } i = \kappa(mj) : P \\ \mathbf{pp(i)} & \text{if } i = \kappa(\sigma) : P \end{cases} \bigstar \lambda z.\eta\,(love(mj, z)))\right)(\kappa(\sigma))$$

[7]A reviewer suggests that giving"perspective sensitive" proper names a different type from ordinary proper names could be seen as an undesirable complication. We could in fact give all proper names uniformly type $\Diamond e$. However, the distinction in type is motivated by the distinction in function between certain uses of proper names in given contexts. The type assignment is relative to a given context, because, as (Asudeh and Giorgolo 2016) point out, whether a name seems to have a double life, like *Peter Parker*, depends on what we assume to be true about the name and its bearer. The type assignment therefore simply reflects this reality (that certain names are 'controversial' and others are not). The reviewer also asks whether P-HYPE has something to say about misunderstanding that can arise in dialogue where dialogue participants understand different referents for a particular utterance of a proper name. This usually happens when not enough information is salient in the conversational context to determine which Mary, or John, etc, is meant. As such, it is more a question about the pragmatic discourse context than about the semantic competence that a name user has, and so we haven't analysed this phenomenon. In P-HYPE each Mary would be associated with a distinct lexical entry, but some Mary's might be associated with two distinct lexical entries, if someone thinks that there are two people corresponding to one Mary. (Asudeh and Giorgolo 2016) discuss such cases and offer a suggested solution.

(7) $love(mj_\sigma, sm(\kappa(\sigma)))$

Since *Spiderman* in (6) scopes above ★ and above κ, it is interpreted relative to the default perspective index, which is the index of the speaker, who they assume in their model to be enlightened. They thus stipulate that the speaker's perspective is the one fed to an expression of the form $a\bigstar f$, which by definition denotes $\lambda i.f(a(i))(i)$, and thus, if the speaker's index is j, we always evaluate some expression of the form $a\bigstar f$ at j.[8] When, however, a perspective relative expression scopes below the function f in $a\bigstar f$, it is caught by the κ operator.

2. P-HYPE: a combination of HYPE and perspective sensitivity

HYPE (Leitgeb 2018) is a logic which employs states/situations.[9] States may be like classical possible worlds, but may also be partial (or *gappy*)–verifying neither a formula nor its negation– and inconsistent (or *glutty*)– verifying a formula and its negation. One nice feature of HYPE is that it behaves entirely classically at a subset of states; as such, linguistic analyses couched in classical logics can be transferred to HYPE. HYPE incorporates special incompatibility $\perp$ and fusion operators $\circ$ in the satisfaction clauses for negation and the conditional, somewhat like (Veltman 1985: pp. 202–7):

1. $\circ : S \times S \to S$ is a partial commutative, associative binary function (called *fusion*), such that:
   - Either $s \circ s'$ is undefined, or $s \circ s'$ is defined (and hence in S) in which case it is required that $V(s \circ s') \supseteq V(s) \cup V(s')$.
   - $s \circ s$ is defined, and $s \circ s = s$.
2. $\perp$ is a binary symmetric relation on S (the incompatibility relation), such that:
   - If there is a v with $v \in V(s)$ and $\bar{v} \in V(s')$, then $s \perp s'$.
   - If $s \perp s'$ and both $s \circ s''$ and $s' \circ s'''$ are defined, then $s \circ s'' \perp s' \circ s'''$.

$\circ$ gives rise to a partial order $\leq$, such that, for all $s, s' \in S$, $s \leq s'$ iff $s \circ s'$ is defined and $s \circ s' = s'$. Importantly, truth is monotonic under fusion extension: for all s, if $s \models A$ and $s \circ s'$ is defined, then $s \circ s' \models A$.
Variable assignments ρ and their modified variants $\rho(d/x)$ behave as in Classical Predicate logic. Satisfaction of a formula ϕ is defined relative to a state and a variable assignment (written: $s, \rho \models \phi$), and the clauses for the logical symbols are as usual, except for $\neg$ and $\supset$, which have a distinctly modal flavour: $s, \rho \models \neg A$ iff for all s' : if $s', \rho \models A$ then $s \perp s'$ and $s, \rho \models A \supset B$ iff for all s' : if $s', \rho \models A$ and $s \circ s'$ is defined, then $s \circ s' \models B$. The reader should consult (Leitgeb 2018) for more details, including the relationship of HYPE to Classical, Intuitionistic and four-valued logic.

2.1. Introducing P-HYPE: a combinination of HYPE and AG's perspective-sensitive semantics

In P-HYPE, we require the usual hierarchy of typed domains familiar from (Gallin 1975), whose elements correspond to different kinds of entities. To this end, let $TYPE$ be the smallest set such that:

[8]The technical stipulation they make is grounded in certain claims about perspective relativity, such as the claim that sentences or expressions which are perspective relative are usually relative to the perspective of the utterer of them, and if they are relative to other perspectives, they are relative either to individuals salient in some group within a given context, or are relative to the perspective of the subject of the sentence. We won't assess these claims here, but suffice to say that they have been discussed and broadly endorsed by researchers working on perspective relativity.

[9]We will use the words 'states' and 'situations' interchangeably.

1. $e, t, p, s \in TYPE$

2. $\alpha, \beta \in TYPE$ implies $\alpha \to \beta \in TYPE$

3. $\alpha \in TYPE$ implies $\Diamond\alpha \in TYPE$

For each type, there is a countable set of constants, and variables, and the set of constants (variables) is the union of the sets of constants (variables) of each type:

- $CON = \bigcup_{\tau \in TYPE} CON_\tau$
- $VAR = \bigcup_{\tau \in TYPE} VAR_\tau$

The set of terms is the union of the sets of terms of type τ, for arbitrary τ:

$TERM = \bigcup_{\tau \in TYPE} TERM_\tau$

The set $TERM_\tau$ for arbitrary type τ is then defined as follows:

- $c \in CON_\tau$ implies $c \in TERM_\tau$;
- $x \in VAR_\tau$ implies $x \in TERM_\tau$;
- $\tau = \alpha \to \beta$, $t \in TERM_\beta$ and $x \in VAR_\alpha$ imply $(\lambda x.t)_\tau \in TERM_\tau$
- $t \in TERM_{\alpha \to \tau}$ and $u \in TERM_\alpha$ implies $(t\, u) \in TERM_\tau$.
- $A \in TERM_t$ and $x \in VAR_\alpha$ implies $(\forall x.A) \in TERM_t$
- $A \in TERM_t$ implies $\neg_c A \in TERM_t$
- $A, B \in TERM_t$ implies $(A * B) \in TERM_t$, for $* \in \{\wedge, \vee, \to\}$
- $x \in TERM_e$ implies $DOX_x \in TERM_{s \to s \to t}$ and $PROV_x \in TERM_{s \to s \to t}$
- $\circ \in TERM_{s \to s \to s}$
- $\leq \in TERM_{s \to s \to t}$
- $\pi \in TERM_{p \to s \to s \to t}$
- $\kappa \in TERM_{e \to s \to p}$
- $\perp \in TERM_{s \to s \to t}$

Suppose we have sets S, D, P, where:

- $S = S_c \uplus S_n \neq \emptyset$, where S_n is the set of glutty or gappy states ('non-classical' states) and S_c is the set of classical states.
- $D \neq \emptyset$ is the domain of individuals
- $P \neq \emptyset$ is the set of perspective indices.

Consider functions κ, π:

- $\kappa : D \to S \to P$, is a function that associates a unique perspective index $\kappa(d)(s)$ to each individual d in a state s. (refinements possible)
- $\pi : P \to S \to \mathscr{P}(S)$ maps every perspective index $\kappa(d)(s) \in P$ and states $s \in S$ to a set of states $\pi(\kappa(d)(s))\,(s) \subseteq S$, the *perspective set* or p-set of d at s. We present π in the term language as a characteristic function of type $P \to S \to S \to \{1, 0\}$.

We also have a distinguished perspective index:

- $E \in P$ is called *enlightened* and is such that for all s, s': $\pi(E)(s)(s')$ iff $s' \in \{s\}$, whence $s' = s$

The (optional) *'privacy' condition of AG*:

- For all $d, d' \in D$ for which $d \neq d'$, and all $s \in S$, $\pi(\kappa(d, s), s) \cap \pi(\kappa(d', s), s) = \emptyset$.

HYPE negation involves $\perp$ and the conditional involves $\circ$, and can be defined directly in our type-theoretic framework, in the object language:

WORD	DENOTATION	ABBREVIATION
Spiderman	$\lambda i, s. \begin{cases} sm(i)(s) & \text{if } \exists s \in S.\, i = \kappa(h, s) \\ pp(i)(s) & \text{else } \exists s \in S.\, i = E \end{cases} : \Diamond e$	sm
Inductive	$\lambda x, \lambda j, s. \begin{cases} I(j)(s)(x(j)) & \text{if } \exists s \in S.\, j = \kappa(h)(s) \\ finite(j)(s)(x(j)) & \text{else } \exists s : S.\, j = E \end{cases} : \Diamond e \rightarrow \Diamond(s \rightarrow t)$	$inductive$
Love	$\lambda y, x, i, s. .\ \forall s'[\pi(i)(s)(s') \rightarrow love\,(i)(s')(x)(y)\,(\kappa(x, s')))] : \Diamond e \rightarrow e \rightarrow \Diamond(s \rightarrow t)$	$love$
Believe/Think	$\lambda p, x, i, s.\forall s'[s \leq s' \wedge \pi(i)(s)(s') \rightarrow$ $\forall s''[DOX_x\, s's'' \rightarrow p\ (\kappa(x)(s''))(s'')]] : \Diamond(s \rightarrow t) \rightarrow e \rightarrow \Diamond(s \rightarrow t)$	$think$
Prove	$\lambda p, x, i, s.\forall s'[s \leq s' \wedge \pi(i)(s)(s') \rightarrow$ $\forall s''[PROV_x\, s's'' \rightarrow p\ (\kappa(x)(s''))(s'')]] : \Diamond(s \rightarrow t) \rightarrow e \rightarrow \Diamond(s \rightarrow t)$	$\lambda p, x, i.prove(i, x, p(\kappa(x, s''))$
the primes	$\lambda i, s.\ \iota x : prime.number\,(i)\,(s)\,(x(i)) : \Diamond e$	$the.primes$

Table 2 Simplified lexical entries

- $(\neg A_{s \rightarrow t}) = \lambda s.\forall s'((A_{s \rightarrow t})(s') \rightarrow s \perp s')$
- $(A_{s \rightarrow t} \supset B_{s \rightarrow t}) = \lambda s.\forall s'(s \leq s' \wedge (A_{s \rightarrow t})(s') \rightarrow (B_{s \rightarrow t})(s'))$

A frame $\mathcal{F} = \langle S, \mathscr{D}, \kappa, P, E, \pi, \circ, \perp \rangle$ based on D, S and P is a family of sets $\mathscr{D} = \{D_\alpha \mid \alpha \in TYPE\}$ such that $D_e = D, D_t = \{1, 0\}, D_s = S$ and $D_p = P$, and $D_{\alpha \rightarrow \beta} \subseteq \{f \mid f : D_\alpha \rightarrow D_\beta\}$ for each type $\alpha \rightarrow \beta$ and $E, \kappa, \pi, \circ, \perp$ are as above. A *P-HYPE* model is a structure $\mathfrak{M} = \langle \mathcal{F}, m \rangle$ where $\mathcal{F}$ is as above and $m : \Pi\alpha.CON_\alpha \rightarrow D_\alpha$ is an interpretation of constants. An assignment over $\mathfrak{M}$ is a function $\rho : \Pi\alpha.VAR_\alpha \rightarrow D_\alpha$. Variable assignments ρ and their modified variants $\rho(d/x)$ (i.e $x \mapsto d$) behave as in Classical Predicate logic. There exists an *admissible* valuation V, which assigns to each assignment ρ over $\mathfrak{M}$ and each term A_α a value $V_a(A_\alpha) \in D_\alpha$, provided the following conditions are met:

- $V_\rho(x_\alpha) = \rho(x_\alpha)$
- $V_\rho(c_\alpha) = m(c_\alpha)$
- $V_\rho(\forall x_\alpha\ A) = \bigcap_{d \in D_\alpha} V_{\rho(d/x)}(A)$
- $V_\rho(\exists x_\alpha\ A) = \bigcup_{d \in D_\alpha} V_{\rho(d/x)}(A)$
- $V_\rho(A_{\alpha \rightarrow \beta} B_\alpha) = V_\rho(A_{\alpha \rightarrow \beta}) V_\rho(B_\alpha)$
- $V_\rho(A_\alpha \equiv B_\alpha) = \{s \mid V_\rho(A_\alpha) = V_\rho(B_\alpha)\}$
- $V_\rho(\lambda x_\alpha A_\beta) =$ the function f on D_α whose value at $d \in D_\alpha$ is equal to $V_{\rho'} A_\beta$, where $\rho' = \rho(d/x)$

2.2. Lexical entries and example

There are three comments to make about these lexical entries in **Table 2**. Firstly, h denotes 'Harold' (who features in our examples), 'E' denotes the enlightened perspective and 'u' denotes the perspective index of the utterer of a sentence. The enlightened perspective index is the perspective index which, if supplied to an expression whose denotation takes a perspective index as an argument, returns the intension of that expression. Secondly, many of these lexical entries are simplified. For example, we are assuming (for expository simplicity) that *prove* is a guarded universal quantifier over worlds–though we haven't specified what sort of universal quantifier it is–and that *Prove* is factive, and so presupposes the truth of its complement. Thirdly, a crucial aspect of the lexical entries for verbs, is that we are able to formalise the intuition of AG that such complements are always interpreted relative to a perspective which the utterer thinks is the perspective of another person. Consider the denotation of *believe*, which combines with a proposition of type $\Diamond(s \to t)$ (i.e, a function from perspective indices to states to truth values), an individual and a perspective index. We assume that, in the case of propositional attitude verbs, this perspective index must always be the utterer's perspective index. Where u is the utterer's perspective index at state s, *Believe* then universally quantifies over both (i) all the states $s' \geq s$, such that $s' \in \pi(u)(s)$, where s is the world in which the sentence is being evaluated and (ii) all the states s'' which are doxastically accessible from $s \circ s'$. x *believes* p is then true iff p is true in s'' relative to the perspective index associated with x at s''.

Consider (8) and (9):[10]

(8) Harold proves that the primes are not inductive.

(9) Harold proves that the primes are infinite.

Using the lexical entries above, we can derive (10) for a sentence like (8) and (11) for a sentence like (9):

(10) $$\lambda s.\forall s' [\, s \leq s' \wedge s' \in \pi(u,s)] \to \forall s''[PROV_x\, s's'' \to \neg I(\kappa(h,s''))(s'')(\iota x.prime.number(x(\kappa(h,s''))))]$$

(11) $$\lambda s.\forall s' [\, s \leq s' \wedge s' \in \pi(u,s)] \to \forall s''[PROV_x\, s's'' \to \neg finite(\kappa(h,s''))(s'')(\iota x.prime.number(x(\kappa(h,s''))))]$$

Crucially, (10) and (11) will differ in truth value, if Harold associates distinct denotations with *inductive* and *finite*.
If we scope both *inductive* and *the primes* above $\bigstar$, we derive ((12)), the interpretation on which both *are not inductive*, and *the prime numbers* are interpreted relative to E and within the p-set of associated with E:

(12) $$(\eta\,(\lambda x, \lambda j, s. \begin{cases} I(j)(s)(x(j)) & \text{if } \exists s \in S.\ j = \kappa(h)(s) \\ finite(j)(s)(x(j)) & \text{else } \exists s : S.\ j = E \end{cases}))\bigstar$$

$$\lambda R.\lambda j, s. \begin{cases} \iota x : prime.number(j)(s)(x(j)) & \text{if } \exists s \in S.\ j = \kappa(h)(s) \\ \iota x : prime.number(j)(s)(x(j)) & \text{else } \exists s : S.\ j = E \end{cases})\bigstar$$
$$\lambda y.not(\lambda i, s.\forall s', s''(s \leq s' \wedge \pi(i)(s)(s') \wedge (PROV_x\, s'\, s'') \to R(\eta(y))(s'')(\kappa(h)(s''))))])$$

Feeding E to (12) reduces to (13) :

(13) $$\lambda s.\forall s''(PROV_x\, s\, s'' \to \neg_c finite(E)(s'')(\iota x.prime.number(E)(s'')(x(E)))]$$

The interpretation on which both *are not inductive*, and *the prime numbers* are interpreted relative to u and within the p-set of associated with u is as follows:

(14) $$\lambda s.\forall s' [\, s \leq s' \wedge s' \in \pi(u)(s)] \to \forall s''[PROV_x\, s's'' \to \neg I(u)(s'')(\iota x.prime.number(u)(s'')(x(u)))]$$

There remain two 'mixed' interpretations:

(15) $$\lambda s.\forall s' [\, s \leq s' \wedge s' \in \pi(u)(s)] \to \forall s''[PROV_x\, s's'' \to \neg I(u)(s'')(\iota x.prime.number(\kappa(h)(s''))(s'')(x(\kappa(h)(s''))))]$$

[10] In (Cresswell 1985: p.82) a set is defined to be 'finite' iff it cannot be put into a one-one correspondence with a proper subset of itself, and a set is 'inductive' iff it can be put into a one-one correspondence with a proper initial segment of the natural numbers. The inductive sets and the finite sets are provably equivalent in ZFC.

(16) $\lambda s.\forall s' [\, s \leq s' \wedge s' \in \pi(u)(s)] \rightarrow \forall s''[PROV_x\, s's'' \rightarrow \neg I(\kappa(h)(s''))(s'')(\iota x.prime.number(u)(s'')(x(u)))]$

Having introduced P-HYPE, we would like to respond to a few remarks made by reviewers. A reviewer asks how well the view of perspectives outlined deals with cases where on one perspective a proper name does not denote at all whereas on other perspectives it does. In P-HYPE any user of a name would, if they can use the name, associate a perspective with the name, even if the user considers the name to be non-denoting. Thus the difference between the two cases depends on whether someone has a metalinguistic belief to the effect that, for example, 'Zeus' denotes. The reviewer asks also how in P-HYPE we can account for someone, let's call her Mary, who considers Jupiter to be identical to Zeus but does not believe that there is such a god. There are various ways we might consider accounting for this, however, we have not decided which is best, and so suggest just one possibility. Suppose that a perspective index can be supplied for certain fictions which are salient in a discourse context, or perhaps certain people's views of those fictions. Then the identity of Zeus and Jupiter would be true relative to the perspective index associated with this fiction in the mind of Mary, and the perspective index supplied for her belief that there are no gods would be her very own dedicated perspective index. This supports the intuition that when we speak truth about fiction, we often do so from within a particular fiction, or from some messy combination of the fiction with other beliefs we have (Lewis 1978).
Another reviewer had trouble seeing what the value of HYPE is in the semantics outlined, and asks how perspectives are acquired and modified. These are good questions, which I attempt to answer in (Burke 2019). Suffice to say that the role of the fusion operator in HYPE actually forms a crucial role in my account, in that it allows us to combine and enlarge perspectives. Thus the HYPE framework is very useful for this. Furthermore, as discussed earlier, the HYPE framework is compatible with the sorts of analyses that semanticists have given of intensional phenomena (for example in (Heim & von Fintel 2011)), which usually employ classical logic.
Finally, the same reviewer questions a perceived 'relativism' that she thinks our semantics entails, by having both the reference of names and predicates as being dependent on a perspective. Here we would like to clarify and expand upon this objection. According to the objection, if we allow predicates to be perspective relative across the board, we predict that sentences like (17) could be true relative to some perspectives, and therefore not plainly false:

(17) There are ten natural numbers.

But this objection misunderstands what we intend by saying something is true relative to a perspective. To say this is simply to say that there exists a speaker whose whose mental model is constituted in such a way as to associate certain representations with certain sentence parts.[11] This is compatible with (17) being plainly false, and the truth/falsity *simpliciter* of a sentence is determined relative to the enlightened perspective index. We are not denying, unlike MacFarlane (2014), that certain sentences are true *simpliciter*. For us, (17) is strictly speaking false, however it is true (or coherent) relative to some bizarre perspective index, which is unlikely to be associated with all but the strangest of individuals, and unlikely to be salient in any context. In fact, in P-HYPE we have E, the dedicated, designated perspective index associated with the enlightened perspective, which allows us to reason about 'plain truth' by simply providing the ordinary intension associated with a sentence constituent. So the charge of relativism is not correct.

2.3. Anaphora in P-HYPE: the State.Set monad

In this final section we will take a quick look at how intra-sentential anaphora can be analysed in P-HYPE.
Consider (18), on the reading in which *he* is anaphoric to *a man she thinks is Peter Parker*:

[11] We could even talk of the *coherence* of a statement relative to a perspective, instead of the truth of a statement relative to a perspective, if this is less liable to confuse.

(18) Mary Jane loves a man she believes is Peter Parker. She believes he isn't Spiderman.

In the standard intensional semantics, at least in which, following (Kripke 1980), co-referring names are given the same semantic value and identity statements are necessarily true or necessarily false, the second sentence of ((18)) denotes the empty set. Clearly, however, there is a sense in which Mary Jane can believe that Spiderman is not Peter Parker. (Lewis 1979) uses centred worlds to account for cases like this, in which someone does not believe a true identity statement and these can potentially be combined with the dynamic semantics of (Groenendijk and Stokhof 1991) in order to model sentences such as (18). Our semantics can also be enriched with a monad that has been used to model anaphora (Charlow 2014): the State Set monad, which is defined as follows:

1. $\Diamond\alpha = R \rightarrow (\alpha \times R) \rightarrow t$
2. $\eta(a) = \lambda r.\{\langle a, r\rangle\}$
3. $m \bigstar \lambda v.\pi = \lambda s.\bigcup_{\langle a,s'\rangle \in m\, s} \pi[a/v]s'$

Here, following (Charlow 2014), R is the set of stacks, which are linear sequences of discourse referents (drefs), and r, r' are variables over stacks. The stack r can be extended with x (written $r\widehat{x}$). The last member of r is the most recently introduced dref, and is notated $r_\top$, such that $(r\widehat{a})_\top = a$. Following (Charlow 2014), we adopt the definitions in (19) (where *pro* is the denotation of a pronoun, which picks out the most recent dref), which allow for indefinites to bind pronouns intra-sententially:

(19) a. $a.man = \lambda r.\bigcup\{\langle x, r\rangle \mid man(x)\}\})$
b. $m^{\triangleright} = m \bigstar \lambda v, r.\eta(v)r\widehat{v} = m \bigstar \lambda v, r.\{\langle v, r\widehat{v}\rangle\}.$
c. $pro := \lambda r.\{\langle r_\top, r\rangle\}$

We can in fact derive (20) from these definitions (see (Charlow 2014:p.47)), which enables a $\triangleright$-shifted m to bind a pronoun in its scope:

(20) $m^{\triangleright} \bigstar \lambda v.pro \bigstar \lambda u.\pi = m^{\triangleright} \bigstar \lambda v.\pi[v/u]$

With these definitions in place (and the fact, *LeftId*, that in any monad $\eta(a) \bigstar f = f\, a$), we can give the semantics of (18) (which we notate $[\![(18)]\!]$) via the first equation in this reduction series below, and we can compositionally derive this lambda term from the parts of (18) (though space reasons precludes us doing so here:[12]

$$
\begin{aligned}
[\![(18)]\!] &= (\eta(mj))^{\triangleright} \bigstar \lambda x.pro \bigstar \lambda x'.pro \bigstar \lambda x''.a.man^{\triangleright} \bigstar \lambda y.pro \bigstar \lambda y'.sm \bigstar \lambda z.pro \bigstar \lambda y''.\\
&\quad \eta[(love(x,y) \wedge think(x', y' = z)), \wedge think(x', y'' \neq sm(\kappa(x')(s''))]\\
&=_{by\,(20)} (\eta(mj))^{\triangleright} \bigstar \lambda x.a.man^{\triangleright} \bigstar \lambda y.\eta(sm) \bigstar \lambda z.pro \bigstar \lambda y''.\\
&\quad \eta[(love(x,y) \wedge think(x, y = z)), \wedge think(x, y'' \neq sm(\kappa(x)(s''))]\\
&=_{by\,LeftId}\ a.man^{\triangleright} \bigstar \lambda y.pro \bigstar \lambda y''.\\
&\quad \lambda r.\{\langle\ [(love(mj,y) \wedge think(mj, y = pp)), \wedge think(m, y'' \neq sm(\kappa(m)(s''))],\ r\widehat{\ }mj\widehat{\ }y\ \rangle\}\\
&=_{by\,(20)}\ a.man^{\triangleright} \bigstar \lambda y, r.\\
&\quad \{\langle\ [(love(mj,y) \wedge think(mj, y = pp)), \wedge think(mj, y \neq sm(\kappa(m)(s''))]r\widehat{\ }mj\widehat{\ }y\ \rangle\}
\end{aligned}
$$

The last member of this sequence, reduces by definition of $\bigstar$ to (21), which consists of a function from stacks to sets of pairs consisting of booleans and stacks updated with the drefs mj and a, if a is a man:

(21) $\lambda r.\bigcup_{\langle a,r'\rangle \in (a.man^{\triangleright}(r))}\{\langle\ [(love(m,y) \wedge think(m, a = pp)), \wedge think(m, a = sm(\kappa(m)(s''))]\ r\widehat{\ }mj\widehat{\ }a\ \rangle\}$

[12] A compositional derivation of this lambda term can be given via higher order continuations, much along the lines that (Barker and Shan 2014) use these to account for multiple pronouns.

3. Conclusion

We have presented P-HYPE and discussed a monadic approach to hyperintensionality. Elsewhere (Burke 2019) we have discussed the role of perspectives in our account, and phenomena such as metalinguistic focus negation. Here we in addition extend our fragment to cover intra-sentential anaphora, and we have responded to some questions that arise in our account of hyperintensionality. In future work we hope to explore the P-HYPE account of hyperintensionality by comparing it with alternative frameworks which are similar in some respects, such as that of truthmaker semantics (Fine 2017).

References

Asudeh, A. and G. Giorgolo (2016). Perspectives. *Semantics & Pragmatics 9*(21), 1–53.

Barker, C. and C.-c. Shan (2014). *Continuations and natural language*, Volume 53. Oxford studies in theoretical linguistics, OUP.

Burke, L. (2019). On P-HYPE: a compositional extension of hype. Analysing hyperintensionality and metalinguistic focus via multiple side effects. *Studia Logica. Trends in Logic XVIII. Logic in High Definition: Developing Fine-Grained Semantics.*

Charlow, S. (2014). On the semantics of exceptional scope. *PhD diss,. New York University.*

Cresswell, M. J. (1985). *Structured meanings.* Cambridge, MA: MIT.

Fairtlough, M. and M. Mendler (1997). Propositional Lax logic. *Information and Computation 137*(1), 1–33.

Fine, K. (2017). Truthmaker semantics. In C. W. B. Hale and A. Miller (Eds.), *A Companion to the Philosophy of Language.* John Wiley & Sons, Ltd, Chichester, UK (online).

Fox, C. and S. Lappin (2008). *Foundations of Intensional Semantics.* Oxford: Blackwell.

Gallin, D. (1975). *Intensional and higher-order modal logic: With applications to Montague semantics*, Volume 19. Elsevier.

Groenendijk, J. and M. Stokhof (1991). Dynamic predicate logic. *Linguistics and philosophy 14*(1), 39–100.

Heim & von Fintel (2011). Intensional semantics: Mit spring 2011 edition. *Retrieved from http://mit.edu/fintel/IntensionalSemantics.pdf..*

Kripke, S. A. (1980). *Naming and Necessity.* Cambride, MA: Harvard University Press.

Leitgeb, H. (2018). HYPE: A system of hyperintensional logic (with an application to semantic paradoxes). *Journal of Philosophical Logic*, 1–101.

Lewis, D. (1978). Truth in fiction. *American philosophical quarterly 15*(1), 37–46.

Lewis, D. (1979). Attitudes de dicto and de se. *The philosophical review 88*(4), 513–543.

MacFarlane, J. (2014). *Assessment sensitivity: Relative truth and its applications.* OUP Oxford.

Shan, C.-C. (2002). Monads for natural language semantics. In *Proceedings of the ESSLLI 2001 Student Session*, pp. 285–298.

Shan, C.-C. (2007). Linguistic side effects. In C. Barker and P. Jacobson (Eds.), *Direct compositionality*, pp. 132–163. Oxford: Oxford studies in theoretical linguistics,.

Veltman, F. (1985). *Logic for Conditionals.* Ph. D. thesis, University of Amsterdam.

Zimmermann, T. E. (2005). What's in two names? *Journal of Semantics 22*(1), 53–96.

Zimmermann, T. E. (2012). Compositionality problems and how to solve them. *Oxford handbook of compositionality*, 81–106.

AUTHOR INDEX

Association for Computational Linguistics
209 N. Eighth Street
Stroudsburg, Pennsylvania 18360

ISBN 978-1-5108-9095-4

CURRAN ASSOCIATES INC.
proceedings.com